THE ART OF SELLING A BUSINESS

Guidebook for Buying or Selling a Business

Jerry S. Horton, Ph.D.

Order this book at www.amazon.com

ISBN-10: 1519210582

ISBN-13: 978-1519210586

For more information

Contact

Jerry S. Horton

Email: jerryshorton@aol.com

Published by Openview Publishing, LLC

Acknowledgements

There are too many people to list here that encouraged me in my journey to the past and so if I miss some please pardon me. The first person I would like to thank is my wife Cynthia who, after reading the manuscript encouraged me to write the book. Without her encouragement and advice I would have never pursued this quest. I also would like to thank Barbara Yates Flewelling for proofing and editing my book, and offering invaluable suggestions. Thank you Barbara.

I also want to give a special thanks to Brenda Halversen who gave me my first business brokering job. Her advice at the beginning was indispensable in my becoming a certified business broker.

Chapter 1 Introduction

Most people do not realize they are able to sell their own businesses.

If you are one of those people, then this is your lucky day. I will teach you that you can, and will also teach you how.

If you hire a broker or if you are a broker, this book will also benefit you. It is concise and addresses the problems and pitfalls associated with selling and buying a business.

It is very important for you, as a business owner or business buyer, to know the information presented in this book.

To begin, here are some important factors you should consider about your business.

- Most businesses go unsold, and not realized as a valuable asset.
- Some people make millions selling their businesses. Your business may have great value in the marketplace.
- Our tax system works against us in keeping and operating a business. Selling a business is a capital gain, which h carries a much lower tax rate than the tax on business income.
- One of the advantages of owning a business is that you can leverage your time by having people work for you. The business builds value and you can sell this value to buyers who are looking for your particular business

- Buying a business will leverage your investment, since it is a way to multiply your return on an investment.
- When selling a business, it is typical to get back a multiple of your original investment.

The same set of skills are necessary for both buying and selling a business, and it is the same set of factors that need to be considered. The knowledge gained from my book will benefit both you as a seller or buyer.

Before you consider selling, there are questions to be answered. Do you really want to sell? Have you really thought this out and is this what you honestly want to do? If the answers are yes, then continue. But, if the answers are "I am not sure," then do not travel this road until all the twists and turns have been considered, and important decisions have been thoroughly studied. You want to successfully arrive at the end of the selling process.

Selling your business is a step by step process that requires you to focus on the end destination at each step. It is not a hard or difficult journey, but it requires patience and knowledge of how to make proceed. This guidebook provides you the roadmap that you will need to follow. It is your guarantee to arrive at your destination successively. Read it and use it as a reference. It will increase your probability of success.

It is important for an owner to maintain the right attitude throughout the whole process. One of the largest roadblocks is that many business owners believe that the business and they are one entity. They believe that without them the business has no value and that no one else can run or operate the business successfully. If you are one of these owners, do not continue further in this book – you will not sell your business. Maybe you should reorganize your company and rethink your operation of it.

A better perspective is to think of the business as being a separate entity of its own, and not an extended part of yourself. You need to believe that it can exist, survive and grow without your being part of it. Your best attitude is to believe that others can learn to run the business, and that the business has great value, even without you. Yes, you may have done a great job in building the business and you may be very talented, but it will require you to work *with* the buyer in learning the business. To someone willing to buy your business, it is important for them to know that the business can operate without you. Once you understand this concept, you can take steps to train others (managers, salesman, etc.) to operate the business themselves. This will put you on the road to success in selling your business

It is important to also understand that selling and buying a business has momentum. Once you begin, things will begin to happen and you need this momentum to stay on course to succeed.

First, establish *why* you are selling. Then, do you know what you will do once you sell your business? Do you have a good reason for selling? You need straight answers to these questions.

Some owners are simply burned out and want to do something different. Many have taken the business to the highest level they can, and it is time for them to change their focus. Retirement, health reasons and simply cashing out equity of the business are other good reasons to sell.

It's important to determine what you are going to sell. Are you selling your entire company, or a portion of your company? Are you just selling the assets in your company? What type of company do you have? Is it LLC, S Corporation, C Corporation or a Partnership? Do you own the company outright, or does someone else have a share in it? Do you need anyone else's permission to sell? These are questions that should be worked out *before* beginning the selling process.

Timing is important. One has to assess the right time to sell a business as well as determining the value of your business. Most owners do not understand that timing is everything in selling their company. Many think about selling when the company is stagnating and not doing well. Actually, the best time to sell is when the company is doing well, making good profits and growing. These are the conditions where you will get the highest value and price for your business. Timing is everything.

You should know that the best barometers of business health are sales volume and seller's cash flow or profits. Sales volume indicates to the buyer if the business is growing, static or declining, and measures how the company is doing in the marketplace against competitors. Seller's cash flow or Seller's discretionary cash flow is the profit plus salary and benefits available to the owner from the business. This is the owner's "take home" before taxes. It is the main driver in determining value and price of your business when you are selling. If there is none of the above, then for all practical purposes you can only sell the assets of your company as liquidation. You want to sell the company as a "going concern" with value in its earning capability.

As we discussed above, we need to determine for how much you can sell your company. This is the critical monetary question. To know this, you will have to know how your business compares to similar businesses that have been sold. You will need to know the future trends in which your business will operate, and the true cash flow profit that the business is earning. Profit is the basis for value.

These are complex questions that you will have to answer. Fortunately, this book provides the tools that will assist you to do just that. You will be able to determine the asking price; a price that will sell your business!

But, before we get started on details – it is important to mention one of the most important rules in selling your business.

Buyers are not ignorant of the business world, so your business must be valued and priced realistically!

Because of this rule a good portion of this book is devoted to valuation of a business.

Here is a last word of advice before moving on. You need to have the right vision. Picture yourself selling your company. Maintain control of your ego. Many sellers, as they go through this journey, begin to get the idea that they might be better off financially keeping their business and making more money. Greed comes into play and manifests itself as Seller's Remorse in selling. If you think you might fit into this category, then stop here. Many sellers forget the simple facts that after they sell, they will no longer have the risk that is associated with owning a company, and they no longer have the work associated with the company.

Be sure you want to sell!

Chapter 2 The Process of Selling a Business

There is a process, or series of steps, in selling a business. It is a process that will require patience all the way through to the end. The business is not sold until the SOLD sign is up, and money has passed hands. Do not try to short cut the process. Each of these steps is described below.

Collect Information In this step you will collect information about your business. The needed information is as follows:

SIC and NAIC code for your business… This defines your business type. You can look this up on the internet.

Financial Data… Your current and historical profit and loss, as well as balance sheets or tax returns.

Description of your business… This is used in advertising a description of how your business operates, and needs to be communicated to a buyer.

Who are your customers? What is your target market? How do you sell the product or service?

History of your business… Owner's history and evolution of the business

By collecting this information and then documenting how your business works, you will have essentially defined the answers that a new owner may need to solve any problems they might face in operating the company.

Evaluate Your Business Determine an honest value for your company to help you arrive at an asking price. This step involves analysis of your financial reports. The objective is to first assess the business profitability and past growth, and then compare these findings to other similar business that have sold. If the valuation meets your expectations, then going to the next step in the process is justified. If not, the process stops here unless you *must* sell due to health, divorce or legal problems.

Determine Selling Options In this step you must determine whether you should sell now or simply wait until sometime in the future.

Identify Best Buyers. In this step you will determine the kind of buyer with whom you expect to come in contact. The buyer may be someone in the same business or an investor. It could be someone who is simply buying a job. You will need to define a buyer's profile, which will give the best combination of terms and price, and will likely make a sale. Then you can identify the buyers who fit that profile.

Profile the Company. Develop a marketing flyer that highlights your business' selling features; a flyer that would be mailed or advertised to targeted buyers, soliciting response inquiries. In this flyer you will communicate why it would be to one's advantage to purchase your company. Included in the flyer should be a list of all the reasons your company is special and desirable to own.

Confidential Business Review. For most medium to large companies a document demonstrating a growth history and strategic value for the buyer needs to be developed. It will discuss the growth of the company and serve as a definition, to both buyer and seller, as to what is being offered.

Market to Buyers. This is the official "launch" of the sale of the business. You will begin advertising. Once buyers respond with inquiries, you will work with them to help them understand the business and educate them as necessary.

Structure Transaction Once a buyer understands the business and wants to pursue acquisition, you will negotiate and structure the deal with the highest value and terms with which you are comfortable. Many times this is accomplished via an email or letter of interest that is nonbinding.

Letter of Intent. Once there is a meeting of the minds that results from negotiations of the material points of the transaction, a letter of intent with the buyer will pave the way to a closing. It is an *agreement put into writing*. It will define price, terms, closing date as well as lay the groundwork for a contract and due diligence of the business.

Due Diligence. In this step the documentation, applications, forms and inspections occur to support the purchase. The buyer will verify your offering. Most of this work is verifying your financial data. The buyer will look at the company books to see they match the financial data you advertised. If the business has been documented well initially, then due diligence proceeds quickly. If the business does not pass due diligence, and that which was advertised does not match the results of due diligence, then price and terms would generally be negotiated or the buyer would cease pursuing acquisition.

Purchase Contract. This is a vast extension of the Letter of Intent with financial terms, warranty and other items that obligate both the buyer and seller. You will work with your lawyer, the buyer and the buyer's lawyer to develop a contract for purchase.

Closing. Once execution of the contract takes place, the transaction is complete.

There are important rules of the road that should be understood. A few of these are listed below. Simply following these rules will help you arrive at your desired destination.

- Define everything up front and honestly.
- Let there be no surprises.
- Know the true value of the business.
- Be Patient.
- Have a good reason for selling.
- Keep things moving.
- Keeping trust between yourself and the buyer is paramount.
- Work together, not against each other

Make sure you have a good reason to sell. Sometimes selling your business is out of your control, such as with divorce, health or other uncontrollable circumstances. You have to ask yourself if this is the right time to sell, or would it be better to keep the business and perhaps sell later? The answer is…you should sell the business when it is at the top of its game, and making a good profit. Some would believe that since it is making so much profit, you should wait. But you will make more money from the sale when your company is at its highest value.

The value of your business is a multiple of your profit. Your profit is multiplied by a multiple, and the multiple is dependent on the type of business category it is in. Since the value is dependent on a multiple of profit then it will also be easier to sell and there will be more buyers from which to choose if you sell when profits are high and projected to be grow higher.

Once you commit to the selling process it is important to maintain momentum and motivation. Don't let it drag out. Make it happen as soon as possible. Unexpected things can happen, so if your business is doing well and you want or need to sell, then you should sell as soon as possible. If you don't keep the process moving it could die out and you won't succeed. You are the driving force to make it happen.

Chapter 3 Business dependency on the owner

Probably the biggest roadblock to selling a business is the attitude of the owner. Many do not think anyone else can run their business. This attitude is the kiss of death when it comes to selling your business. It is your job to change both your attitude and your company to be able to operate without you. Here are some of the things you can do.

- Simplify the processes in your business.
- Train employees to do your job.
- Establish management. Don't do it all yourself.
- Delegate tasks.
- Automate accounting and bookkeeping.
- Systemize business processes.
- Stop being a micromanager. Institute a management structure.
- Keep documentation. Have an operations manual and good records.
- Make the effort to have good customer relations.
- Establish a customer service function with which to deal with customers.
- Create a sales function in the company, so the company is not dependent upon you for its sales.
- Keep your state of mind to have the business run without you.
- Have a business plan.
- Strive to show profits, growth and stability.
- Sell the business when it is growing. Timing is everything.

There are many other ways to make your company less dependent upon you. You need to change now, before you sell your company. It is easier than you think.

Remember that possibly the most important rule you will need to know is to make sure the buyer knows that he or someone besides yourself can operate and manage the business.

Chapter 4   What are buyers looking for?

Knowing for what customers are looking for is critical to operate your business. It means running your business by understanding your customers and your product or service. Operate your business to meet the customer needs. The same holds true for selling your company. Know your buyers.

Remember that when selling your business, your buyer is looking to buy your business, not you. You must create the perception that the business can be run without you. So this is one of the most important sales principles in selling your business. Buyers are looking to buy businesses that don't depend on the owner.

As a corollary to this, buyer's want businesses that are fully staffed and managed without the owner or with minimal owner participation. Buyers want an owner who is willing to stay and help the buyer learn the business during the transition of ownership. You must be willing to help operate the company for a sufficient period of time.

Buyers are looking for flexibility on deal structure. You must be creative and open minded. Many sellers begin by demanding a cash deal. While this may happen, the statistics show that most transactions are more complex than a simple cash deal and most sellers have to do some seller financing.

Buyers want a company with a good consistent cash flow. Many times companies may have good cash flow but because of the accounting it is not obvious on the bottom line of the financial statement. It is important to demonstrate through good accounting how much profit the company makes. The accounting may not reflect true profits received by the owner. Owners will operate their companies in a manner to minimize taxes but when you sell your company you need maximize your profits. This strategy will greatly increase the price you will get for your company. The value of the business is a multiple times the profit and has nothing to do with the money you may have saved in taxes in the past.

Your company must have capacity for growth. The buyer must perceive an inherent ability to grow the business. This is one of the main reasons the buyer is pursuing acquisition of a company. Growth is a key factor in the buyer's criteria for purchase.

The owner must communicate a good reason for selling. Reasons such as retirement and health are common. Many owners sell because they are ready to do something else. Regardless of the reason the buyer must be given the confidence that this is a successful business that can be grown and not a business where there is no future.

The buyer must believe that buying a company is a manageable risk. Every business contains some level of business risk and financial risk. The key is that this risk must be manageable and is something with which the buyer can live. No one wants a "bad investment."

The buyer must perceive that the business is systemized, and the success of the company is due to the owner creating a system for dealing with customers, managing the employees, as well as their products. A systematic process insures that success is repeatable each day when the owner leaves the business.

Chapter 5 The Basic Listing

The Basic Listing or Confidential Memorandum is the way you communicate the offer to sell. It is the FOR SALE sign. It is the first thing that needs to be done. It also defines what you want to do. It is the beginning of the process of selling. A list of the types of information it contains is shown below.

- Defines what is being sold
- Contains the price and what is for sale
- Defines Real Estate price or lease amount
- Contains Contact information
- Reason for sale
- High Level Summary Financial Data
- Defines Assets and Liabilities
- Defines Inventory
- Defines Accounts Receivable and Payable
- Defines type of business (SIC or NAICS Code)
- Description of Business
- Byline to attract the buyer
- Type of sale – asset or stock
- Defines whether seller will hold paper or not
- Number of employees and supervisors
- When the business started
- Business organization type - C , S , LLC

Once you know that you are going to sell, how much value the business has, and what you will ask for the business then it is important that you document in writing exactly what you are selling. There can be no "meeting of the minds" between buyer and seller without a definitive statement of what is for sale. This is where the confidential memorandum (listing) comes into play. It is the specification or that which you are selling.

The memorandum can be presented numerous ways. For medium to large businesses, those over $1,000,000 in value, this takes the form of a formal written document. For small to medium businesses, especially ones that are less than $1,000,000, the memorandum takes the form of a spreadsheet. In either case you have to describe the business and what is does.

Golden Rule -This rule should never be violated – never, never say anything bad about the business that is being sold when communicating with a buyer.

It is always best to be silent rather than say anything bad or negative about the business. Let the buyer formulate their own opinions about a business from the information that has been provided. Your job is to have the buyer formulate positive, good thoughts only. Remember, until after you close on the sale, you are still trying to sell your business!

The most important components of the memorandum are:

- Business Description (here is where you must sell the business with words.)
- Business Name and location (only if it is not confidential.) Type of business – SIC code or NAICS code Business Type – S Corp, C Corp, etc...
- Type of Sale – Asset Sale or Stock Sale or Liquidation or portion of the company.

- General location – state, location within the state.
- Number of employees.
- Number of managers or supervisors.
- Something about the organization. How is it organized?
- Basic Historical and Forecast financial data
- What comes with the sale – Receivables, Payables, Liabilities,
- Inventory, Cash and Assets.
- Lease or Purchase of property for the business.
- The price of the business and what are payment terms.
- Terms of a noncompeting agreemen.t
- Training to the buyer that you are offering.
- Options you will accept – seller financing, contingencies, etc.… Why you are selling – 'burn out' is best explained as 'pursuing other interests.'

It is extremely important that the financial data that is contained in the memorandum be accurate and thorough. This is what you have advertised that the company has done, and may do in the future. If it is not accurate and a buyer moves forward, then if the true data be revealed in the due diligence step and does not match that which was advertised, the buyer will rightfully terminate acquisition. You will have wasted the buyer's time and your time. So be accurate and thorough with financial data. It will make the whole process go much more smoothly.

A word about cash flow (profits.) One of the most important selling points of your company is the cash flow it can generate for the buyer. Buyers look at past history. They look at what the business is doing now, and where the market is predicting the cash flow will be when they own the company.

Cash flow is defined as Profit or Net Income, and interest paid, plus depreciation, your salary and your benefits. (Benefits being any money you took out of the company for your personal benefit.) The result is sometimes called discretionary cash flow or adjusted EBITDA (Earnings before taxes and interest and depreciation.)

Interest is added back to profit since the buyer will not have this interest to pay. The business is usually bought debt free meaning the company debt is paid off at closing. Depreciation is added back, since for most companies it is not an actual cash expense, and is there for tax purposes. Your salary is added back since it is a profit you are personally making. For most small companies, this is how the owner's salary is handled, and for medium to large companies only the owner's excess salary can be added back.

Finally, your benefits are those expenses you took out of the company. It may be expenses for your health insurance, personal use of a car or telephone or excess rent. The list goes on and on. The important point about these expenses is that they all have to be accounted for somewhere in your accounting system during the buyer's due diligence. They cannot be made up without proof and they cannot be unaccountable cash that has been taken out of the company.

It is also important to know that this is the written statement of why someone should be interested in and wish to purchase your business. Be sure to include marketing and sales descriptions in your advertisement, and then add your own sales pitch on why this is a great business. Be a salesman!

Once the memorandum is completed it will be your vehicle to communicate to the buyer what you are selling. The more thorough you make this memorandum, the more reliable will be the response from buyers. Your objective is to solicit only buyers that are truly interested and informed; not just "tire kickers."

It is extremely important that you know that selling a business is not the same as selling real estate, a car or a boat. Buyers are making important life decisions and they are not just swayed by a salesman's personality. The data in the memorandum that you convey must be accurate and thorough. They seek the facts and the truth. They need to be shown a vision of owning and operating your business. At the same time, they need to have a level of trust and confidence that the deal will work for them.

Chapter 6 Confidentiality

Above all…. keep it confidential! Customers and employees don't need to know the business is for sale until it's time to tell them.

Before giving any details about the business, you must have the buyer sign a Confidentiality Agreement. This the best way to keep all your discussions confidential. Have buyers sign a Nondisclosure Agreement (NDA) before discussing the business with them. It asks the buyer to keep the information that you share with them confidential, and by signing, the buyer agrees to this. Once they sign an NDA then you can reveal details about the business.

The NDA states the buyer cannot contact employees directly and cannot show the information about the business with others. Neither can they use the information you supply to compete with the business. The NDA states ALL information about the business will be kept confidential.

If there is a violation of the NDA, typically a letter from your attorney to the buyer or buyer's attorney will suffice to make the buyer follow the agreement. These violations are typically a rare event.

As the owner, you may wish to inform only key employees who will need to stay with the company. Usually, it is best to wait until the last steps in the acquisition to get the employees involved. Generally, if employees know too early in the transactions, it will be a distraction from their work and be a de-motivator. This is stress you do not need when you are selling your company. When the business is sold and about to close, then employees can be told. "A need to know" is the key phrase to keep in mind during the acquisition process.

Then, why it is a good idea to keep the sale of the business confidential?

- Discovery may disrupt work, employee morale and the work environment for employees.
- Competitors could use this information against you.
- Customers may get worried and you could potentially lose them. After the sale, customers can be informed of the change. They should be advised that it will be "business as usual" and that their service and quality of product will stay the same or may improve.
- Vendors may be uneasy with the fact that your business is being sold.

Advertising must be done for a "generic company" without revealing name or specific location. Many times buyers will inquire and ask for details either by email or phone. You must have them sign an NDA before sending the detailed information. It is also wise to have the buyer send a buyer prequalification profile describing the assets he or she has to be able to purchase the business. If they do not send this requested information, or if their financial assets do not appear to be sufficient to purchase the business, then do not send the business' detailed information.

In some businesses there may be key employees who will have talk with the buyer before the transaction is complete. You will need to discuss the acquisition with those employees at some time in the overall process. The buyer will want assurances that the employee/employees will stay. This usually happens at the point of contract finalization and as a last step once you, as a seller, are fairly sure that the transaction will happen.

There are support people associated with the business and the buyer will also have support personnel. These people need to know about the sale. Your attorney, your accountant, stockholders in your company and your bookkeeper will have to know you are selling. These are the team of people whom you will need to call upon to get the business sold.

Similarly, once a buyer has signed an NDA, then he or she will no doubt have to share information with his or her accountants and lawyers.

When an NDA is sent to a buyer it is important you solicit prequalification information about the buyer. This includes the following:

- Buyer contact information: Name, address, cell telephone and email address.
- Buyer verification: You will need their driver's license and a picture of the license to be sure they are whom they claim to be.
- Buyer Prequalification: Home address, present occupation and company with whom presently employed.
- Maximum "cash down" available.
- When the buyer is able to close on the business and take possession.
- What type of "deal structure" the buyer would propose.

- Will the buyer need financing and how much?
- Special training qualifications of the buyer and remarks the buyer wishes to share.

One of the reasons you will need the buyer's verification is that there is a history of con men posing as buyers of companies. The way these con men work is to convince the seller to hold a "seller note." Then, at closing before paying their down payment, they get the seller to sign the closing papers. At that point the company is theirs. The con man convinces the seller that the down payment funds are being wired, and that they will arrive later in the afternoon or the next day. Once the closing papers are signed, the con man then factors (sells) the accounts receivable, using a factoring service and then strips the company of its liquid assets. Many owners have lost their companies with this scheme. This has been a common occurrence in recent years.

An important precaution in avoiding con men is to get a copy of the license with the NDA, so you know and can verify who the buyer is at the closing of the transaction. The attorney handling the closing should require driver's licenses from buyer and seller to verify identity. Of course, if you get the driver's license with a picture at the time you get an NDA, then there will be plenty of opportunity to verify the identity of the buyer and the "con" should never reach the point of closing.

Watch out and be careful with buyers. When it does not *feel right*, then it probably is *not* right.

One last word on confidentiality. When dealing with buyers, be businesslike. If that doesn't work, then it is ok to be firm and set the buyer straight as to the rules of the acquisition. Sometimes, one cannot be nice and maintain these necessary rules of confidentiality.

Chapter 7 Buyer Prequalification

This truly is one of the most difficult and important tasks in the whole process. One does not want to work with a buyer who does not have the capability to purchase the business. But there are several places during the process when you can qualify a Buyer.

The first time is when you send the NDA in response to an inquiry. As we discussed previously, the NDA will contain questions to help you assess the buyer's financial position and his or her ability to purchase the business. One of the problems with this method is that Buyers don't fill out that part of the NDA properly. Some may actually fill in false information just so they can see the details of the business. Once you receive a filled out NDA, you have to make a judgment call whether this buyer has the capability to buy your business. If you feel they did not fill out the data correctly, then email or call them and tell them that you need more financial information to prequalify them, or simply tell them with the information that has been sent, you cannot prequalify. You will not send details to the buyer until they have been successfully prequalified. You can use Google search engine in order to research the buyer. It is an invaluable tool in this process.

Remember that just because someone signs an NDA and fills out the prequalification information, it does not mean you have to send them detailed information or any information at all. You must make a judgement if this person is prequalified. Sometimes if you are unsure you can send them summary information until you learn more about the buyer.

The second and no doubt the most important point of prequalification is when the buyer has made an offer. You must require that the buyer submit a proof of funds before you begin negotiating their offer. You should require bank statements or reports of their investments to assess this. You will also need to know how they intend to use these funds to make the purchase. You may even require a letter of credit from their bank or perform a credit report check of the buyer. This is no doubt the most important step in prequalification because both you and the buyer will be spending money on lawyers and accountants during this phase of acquisition for due diligence and contract development. It makes no sense to spend this money and time if the buyer is truly not qualified to purchase the business.

Here is a summary of information you may need to check out a Buyer.

- If it's a company, then check with websites and their customers.
- Secure a Buyer Financial Statement and Bank Statement.
- Buyer's Tax Return.
- Buyer's Credit History.
- Career Resume: Check out his or her history.
- Ask for References.
- Ask to see licenses, if required by business.
- Check out Litigation History, if possible.

Some of this information can be looked at early in the process, and if the buyer is serious in making an offer, more of it can be requested as you move forward.

The third and final place for you to check the Buyer's qualification is contract signing. Contract signing may occur on the day of closing or may occur before that date, and at that time you should require a nonrefundable deposit by the buyer. The rest of the payment due at closing.

Some buyers will try to purchase your business with the least amount down, and at closing, ask you to finance the rest. They will try to negotiate the bulk of payment to be paid over time as a seller note. When you consider this situation, you realize that the buyer is using the profits of your business to buy your business! This can be a tenuous situation, particularly if the buyer does not run your business properly and it fails, resulting in their inability to pay you. Most sellers remedy this situation by requiring at least 60% paid on closing, and some will not accept a seller note. In some cases, you may require the buyer to pledge external collateral outside the business. At least then, if the business fails, you can receive the rest of the payment from selling the external collateral. Of course, many buyers have the option of applying for a loan at a bank. Many may qualify for a SBA loan. This is sometimes a better option than seller financing.

In any case, cash is king and you, as a seller, will have choices to make in to whom you sell. Be careful. There are dangers in qualifying the wrong buyer, and remember, it takes time to sell a business – be patient.

Chapter 8 Psychology of a Deal

There is a mentality associated with the process of selling a business and composure that can greatly aid you. This section contains advice in dealing with the psychological dynamics of selling your company.

First of all, once again, be patient! It is a slow, methodical process. Persistence is an important virtue in this process. Roadblocks can appear and re-appear. You need to work together, with the buyer, to overcome them.

Perceptions are everything. The best of intentions can sometimes give the wrong perceptions. Give the buyer the right one. Make sure communications are straight forward and accurate. Trust between buyer and seller is paramount.

Know where you are at all times in operating your business. Have updated financials, schedules and customer lists to know where your business is operating at all times. It may take a while for the business to sell, perhaps six to nine months, so it must continue to perform as expected during this time period.

Be organized for acquisition. Know what is needed and then collect it. Have it ready to communicate. Acquisition has to be an important priority if you want the sale to happen. Make it your first priority.

Once the deal is set, move as quickly as possible. There are many ways a deal can die, especially if it drags on.

Be motivated to sell. Know who or what the deal killers may be. Know what to negotiate. It is your decision to sell. The deal must make sense to you because you are the decision maker. Make your own decisions on the deal and assess the risk. Once you have set the terms and agreed to them, then let the accountants do the accounting and the lawyers do the legal work. Don't try to be a lawyer or accountant.

When is a deal done?

The deal is only done when it closes. Until that point, there can always be negotiation up to and until the point of closing. Remember, you are still in the process of "selling" to the buyer. There are instances where buyers or sellers did not show up at the closing, having changed their minds at the last moment.

Is there a buyer point of no return? Is there a point where we lose the buyer and we cannot get him or her back? Some buyers may reach a point where they cannot continue. Many times it is almost impossible to turn them around, and yet there are those times it can be done. Sometimes the buyer's perception is simply incorrect and can be changed by more effective communication.

The "wiggle" is when a buyer, or seller, tries to wiggle out of the deal at the last moment. The wiggle is more common than one would expect. For the seller and buyer, these are extremely difficult decisions and can be charged with emotion. With this mix, either one, at the last moment, can try to remove themselves from the deal. Watch out for the wiggle.

Here are some points to remember.

- When do you stop negotiation? The answer is never.

- When do you stop selling? The answer is also never.

- Why is a Letter of Intent needed? It defines the path to the contract.

- What does it mean to negotiate in good faith? The buyer and seller are earnestly trying to make a deal to go through with the acquisition.

What are the points upon which to agree? Sometimes when the negotiation is stalled, the seller and buyer, together, can review the points to which they agree, and keep the negotiations in perspective….and seek to continue. Many times negotiations can drag on, dwelling on minor points that both buyer and seller need to understand. This can be resolved with patience and more effort.

What is the value? Are the buyer and seller dealing with reality? Both buyer and seller need to operate on the basis of the reality of the worth of things. Both have to understand the financial data, the valuation and the characteristics of the business. Only if both operate on this basis will the transaction be successful.

Psychology plays an important role in selling and buying a business. If you are aware of this, then it helps to navigate to a successful end.

Chapter 9 Quick Tips for Sellers

- If it makes sense to develop or have products, then develop them. Some buyers are looking for companies that have products.
- Spend money on R&D and product development, or development of new products and services.
- Can it run without you? Make sure it can.
- Do you have management in place? Eliminate the dependence on you, the owner.
- Are all the profits accounted for? How can you convince a buyer of your true profit?
- Don't sell yourself. Sell your company. That's what buyer is buying.
- Be willing to stay on for a sufficient period of time after the closing.
- Be flexible on deal structure, at same time be creative.
- There are many ways to make a deal.
- Be patient. Selling your company is a slow, methodical process.
- Have a marketing and business plan. Know where your business can go.
- Have an organized, dedicated sales staff. Remember the company cannot run without sales.
- Know where you are at all times. What is your profit, and what is the value of the company?
- Sell when your company is growing not when it is on a downturn.

Chapter 10 People involved in Selling Your Business

There will be a number of people involved in selling your business, and each has a role to fill, and a time of need. You can see the relationships of the people below.

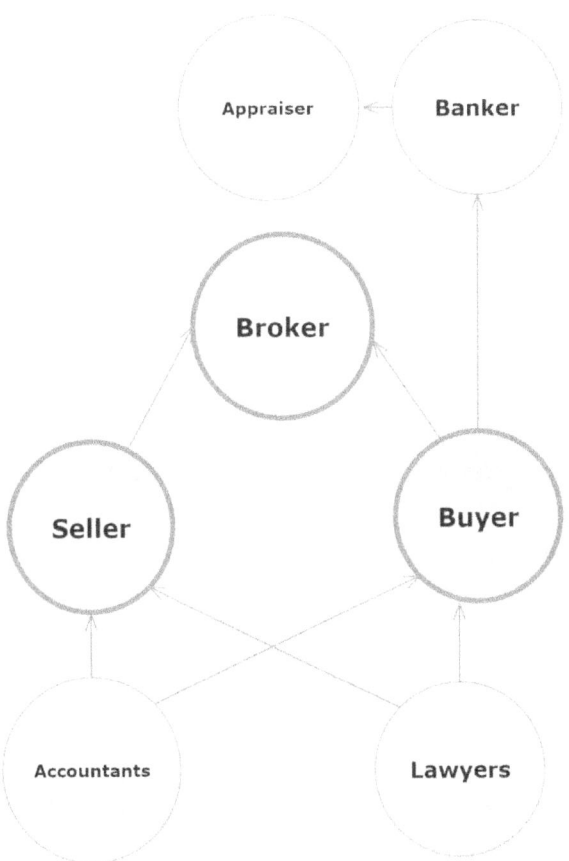

The seller, the buyer and the broker (if you have one) will be there throughout the process. Both seller and buyer will need support of accountants and lawyers. If the buyer intends to finance any part of the purchase, he may need a banker, and the banker may need a property appraiser or business appraiser, or both.

Lawyers are used to draft and review all legal agreements including the Letter of Intent and Purchase Agreement. It is critical that the seller use an attorney for support on these documents. However, you as a buyer or seller, are hiring the attorney for legal advice not business advice. Be sure your attorney knows this.

The accountant is needed to prepare the financial information the seller needs to advertise, and to sell the business. No doubt, he will also be required to support the due diligence phase of acquisition. If you are a buyer, you may have your accountant review the accounting information provided with the offering. Both buyer and seller will also need an accountant in the due diligence step to help verify the financial information.

The appraiser may be needed by the seller, and by the bank, if there is financing involved. If you are selling property with the offering, the seller will need a commercial appraisal of the property. If the bank is financing the purchase of the property, then they will need a property appraisal also, and may need a business appraisal if a portion of the business is financed.

There may be others involved, including escrow agents and closing agents or title companies. But these are the main players in the acquisition process.

Chapter 11 Basis for Value

It is important to understand the basic concepts of value before you put your business on the market, or before considering buying a business.

There are different types of value for an asset. Here are the most common definitions which are used as standards of value.

- Investment Value: Value to a particular buyer or investor.
- Intrinsic Value: Not a standard of value – it is the underlying value based on perception of its usefulness
- Fair Value: Rarely used and rarely do we have a willing seller. It is a definition used in court cases and it is a legal meaning associated with value
- Fair Market Value: It is the one we use in valuing a business for sale in the open market, and is defined below.

The definition of Fair Market Value is that:

- We have both a motivated buyer and seller.
- The buyer and seller are hypothetical and not specific parties.
- The buyer and seller are well informed and advised.
- Both buyer and seller are acting in their own self best interests.
- No synergies considered for either the buyer or seller.
- Payment is made in cash, financing is not considered.
- The business has been on the market for a reasonable time.
- There is no consideration for future events.

Premise of Value is that the business is a going concern and is expected to operate. We are not looking at the business for its liquidation value, as if it were to be closed.

Most companies are sold as ongoing concerns. This means that they are profitable and are expected to be profitable in the future. They are not sold on the basis of assets, but on the basis of their earning power. The value of these businesses is based on how much profit they expect to earn.

Profit is defined as that part of the income that is available to the owner. This may be cast into a net cash flow, or discretionary cash flow, available to the owner. If one uses net cash flow, then using a rate of return or discount rate, one can estimate the value. If using discretionary cash flow, then comparable business sales can be used to estimate value.

We are going to focus on businesses that are ongoing concerns, and we are only talking about Fair Market Value when we discuss valuation.

Chapter 12 Financial Statement

It is important to know how financial statements are created. They are the yardstick we use to measure business profits and value of the company.

The function of the Financial Statement is to report company profit for tax purposes and for control of operating costs. It is a basic accounting summary of the company's performance. Its purpose is to show the profitability as a series of steps and to show the important financial variables as of a financial statement.

Below are the basic accounting equations that drives the financial statement.

Gross Profit = Sales – Cost of Goods

Net Income = Gross Profit - Expenses

The main input is the company's sales. If the company has products or services, and there are direct costs for these products and services. These costs are accumulated into the cost of goods. Some companies do not have direct costs, or do not account for them, so they do not have cost of goods in their financial statement.

Subtracting the cost of goods from the sales results in the gross profit. Gross profit does not account for expenses required to operate the company. Gross profit is the residual profit after sales minus costs associated with production. It represents income before expenses.

Gross profit minus expenses is the profit of the company (prior to taxes) and is net income. It is the profit for purposes of business valuation and is the before tax net income.

The general approach is to make a comparison to other similar companies that have been sold. Using the net income and the statistics of similar companies that have been sold, an estimate of value for the subject company. The analysis is done with the before tax net income rather than the after tax net income because each buyer will have a different tax profile. Taxes cannot be considered because the valuation would not be for the overall market; it would then be a valued based on a specific assumed tax for the company.

The net income reported in the financial statement is not necessarily the income the owner receives while running the business. Let's call this the real cash flow or the cash flow the owner will receive from the company.

Our objective is to determine the real cash flow the owner will receive from owning the business. This profit is called the Seller's Discretionary Cash Flow (SDCF).

A detailed example of the Income Financial Statement is shown on the following page. It shows three years of data with the detailed expenses.

When analyzing these statements, it is normal to look at three years of reports. The purpose of studying three years it to detect trends in expenses and profitability, and to assess how the company might perform in the future.

Sample Income Statement showing three years of data. The bottom line is the Seller's Discretionary Cash Flow that is the real profit earned by the owner. As can be seen below, the Gross Profit is the Sales minus the Cost of Goods. Net Income is the Gross Profit, minus Expenses and adjustments to the Net Income. This reflects the owner's benefits and salary, arriving at the Seller's Discretionary Cash Flow, the real profit to the owner.

Account	2006	2005	2004
Sales	787,185	749,700	714,000
Total Revenues	787,185	749,700	714,000
Cost of Goods	476,942	454,230	432,600
Total Cost of Goods Sold	476,942	454,230	432,600
Gross Profit	310,244	295,470	281,400
Expenses			
Payroll	96,606	91,453	87,099
Advertising	27,000	25,650	25,478
Rent	41,000	39,770	38,577
Insurance	5,623	8,030	9,055
Credit Card	13,072	11,500	10,499
Bookkeeping	2,500	2,406	1,700
Due and Subscriptions	865	850	776
Depreciation	4,200	4,200	4,200
Freight	14,000	13,734	10,401
Maintenance	1,900	1,956	1,638
Officers' Salaries	64,000	59,000	57,000
Shop Supplies	1,054	900	347
Telephone	5,883	5,700	5,956
Payroll taxes	10,078	9,462	9,200
Utilities	8,174	7,636	7,349
Interest Expense	4,948	4,690	4,523
Total Expenses	300,323	286,937	273,798
Net Income Before Taxes	9,920	8,533	7,602
Adjustments			
Officers Compensation	64,000	59,000	57,000
Personal use of telephone	1,200	1,200	1,200
Medical Insurance for owner	1,000	1,000	1,000
Gasoline	960	960	960
Rent Adjustment	-6,150	-5,966	-5,787
Add Depreciation	4,200	4,200	4,200
Add Interest	4,948	4,690	4,523
Total Adjustments	70,158	65,085	63,096
Discretionary Cash Flow	80,078	73,617	70,699

The other important financial statement is the balance sheet. The balance sheet shows the assets and liabilities of the company. It also shows the equity invested and retained by the company. It is used by the buyer to assess how much hard assets, such as equipment, furniture and fixtures, come with the company in its purchase.

	2006	2005	2004
Assets:			
Current Assets			
Checking	89,447	78,361	47,489
Total Inventory	153,753	153,165	150,275
Prepaid Insurance	8,608	8,501	8,139
Total Current Assets	251,808	240,027	205,903
Fixed Assets			
Vehicles	20,000	20,000	20,000
Furniture and Fixtures	92,303	82,602	100,074
Total Fixed Assets - Cost	112,303	102,602	120,074
Accum. Depreciation	-79,690	-81,679	-77,127
Total Fixed Assets - Net	32,613	20,923	42,947
Total Assets	284,421	260,950	248,850
Liabilities			
Current Liabilities			
Accounts Payable	124,227	121,953	110,077
Short Term Note	78,353	63,703	69,878
Total Current Liabilities	202,580	185,656	179,955
Total Liabilities	202,580	185,656	179,955
Equity			
Equity	50,000	50,000	50,000
Retained Earnings	31,841	25,294	18,895
Total Equity	81,841	75,294	68,895
Total Liabilities and Equity	284,421	260,950	248,850

Chapter 13 Special Financial Considerations

Before discussing valuation of a business it is important to review the characteristics of the financial data that is used to develop the financial reports.

Multiple Years of Data

A buyer will be most interested in the current year to date and will want to see how your profits and expenses have changed over time by looking at past years of financial data. A buyer will need to consider:

- The current year or last full year. This is the most important.
- Year to date. For some businesses this may not be as relevant since the business might be seasonal or not uniform throughout the year
- Past Years. A prospective buyer will want to see at least three years of data.

By reviewing past years, the buyer will detect trends and anomalies in expenses. The buyer will try to determine if the business is improving and growing. There may be nonrecurring expenses that do not occur year to year. These expenses have to be reconciled out of the financials since the buyer will be trying to forecast how the company will perform in the future on a normal basis.

At times, buyers want year to date statements in order to see how the company is currently doing, and to forecast the financial performance for the end of the year. There are a number of pitfalls in doing this.

- Cyclic seasonal nature of the business.
- Timing of projects in construction.
- Inaccurate accounting of interim statements.
- The timing of the business sales during the year.

If the business is seasonal in nature, then a simple linear extrapolation to the end of the year will be inaccurate. One has to look at seasonal monthly data from previous years to see what the seasonal pattern is and to use that as a basis of forecasting.

If it is a project oriented company, then forecasting financial performance can be even more difficult. One has to look at the projects in progress, the bids for new projects that may be won, and the accounts receivable for work that has already been completed. Only then will a forecast be accurate. In these types of companies, the buyer is looking at the mix of small and large projects and the success record over time, as well as the detailed project work in progress.

If you are a buyer it is important to evaluate the current year's performance in order to assure yourself that the company is on track. This, compared to past performance, will tell if the trend is indicating a growth.

Accrual versus cash basis of accounting

The cash basis and the accrual basis are the two primary methods of tracking income and expenses in accounting.

One way to explain this, is to say that in the cash basis you do not account for sales until you receive payment, where as in the accrual method sales are accounted for when the sale is made or booked or ordered. In most companies there is a delay between booking the sale and receiving the actual payment.

The accrual method records income items when sales are earned and records deductions when expenses are incurred not when the actual payment is made. For a business invoicing sold items, or work done, the corresponding amount will appear in the books even though no payment has yet been received. Using this method debts owed by the business are shown as they are incurred, even though they may not be paid until much later.

The cash method is the more commonly used method of accounting in small businesses. Under the cash method, income is not counted until cash (or a check) is actually received, and expenses are not counted until they are actually paid. Many times companies will use the cash basis of accounting to minimize forthcoming income taxes.

For business valuation, accrual accounting does provide a truer picture of the business performance than the cash method. If the business is worth more when looking at accrual, then the business is worth more – theoretically. This happens when a company is growing and accounts receivables are growing. Cash accounting does not capture the growth in accounts receivable as revenue, though generally accepted accounting principles would say it is revenue that should be accounted.

Cash accounting is not a good method on which to base valuations. It often doesn't measure the true revenue and earning power of the business, and instead measures how creative or aggressive the owner was in minimizing their taxes.

Accrual accounting more accurately measures the true activity of a business. Revenue is recognized and is shown on the profit and loss statement after the work is completed, a service is performed or a product is delivered, not when the money comes in. Similarly, cost is recognized when you buy something, not when you pay the bill.
For these reasons business appraisers are taught to use accrual based accounting for valuations, and to convert financial statements from cash to accrual when possible. Many business brokers, however, are somewhat perplexed on the differences between cash and accrual, or don't want to spend the time to make the adjustments. Quite often, there isn't a significant difference. For a mature, stable business without a lot of tax manipulations, they can be very close.

For some businesses there is a *huge* difference. A growing business usually has a growing amount of account receivables. Sometimes a dramatic amount, since a high growth period also can be a chaotic and challenging time, with focus not placed on collections. Cash basis accounting doesn't capture all of this growth, and a broker can cost a business owner a lot of money by not accounting for this in his valuation.

Financial Ratios

It will be important to the buyer that he or she can assess where the business is heading and what it will look like in the coming year, after the purchase has been completed.

Financial Ratio calculations are provided in subsequent Chapter 44. These ratios allow us to evaluate the financial performance of a business compared to other companies. You can perform this analysis using RMA data. Founded in 1914, The Risk Management Association (RMA) is a not-for-profit, member-driven professional association whose sole purpose is to advance the use of sound risk principles in the financial services industry.

You can use RMA data to compare your company's financial ratios with other companies of the same type. It provides a grade card for the financial performance of your company. With this data you can see how a business compares to the industry.

You should be concerned about how expenses have changed over time. By examining these expenses, you can see where the company is going and how its future profitability will be impacted. You, as a buyer, can ask questions to the seller as to why expenses are changing, in order to understand what is happening within the business.

Forecasting the future

Businesses are bought on the basis the future not for the past. Buyers are mainly concerned with assessing future performance of the business. Sometimes the past is an indication of the future but not always. Many use the last year's financial information, combined with the year to date financial information, along with the trend in sales to predict the future financial performance of the company.

Here are some tips for the buyer for forecasting.

- Ask the seller what he or she thinks the current year's sales will be. Generally sellers have a good idea what it will be from their past experience.
- Look at the trend in sales over the past three years.
- Study the trends in the industry for similar types of business.
- Use the year to date financial P&L's to model what is currently happening in the company.
- Use this data and the last year's financial data to predict the current year's earnings.

Once you predict the future financial performance you can use these results to value the business.

Beyond this forecasting the seller should be asked how he or she would grow the business if they kept it. A buyer may have your own ideas on how to grow the business, but many times the seller will have a better idea of what it takes.

These are important considerations that should be used in evaluation of the future potential for the business.

Chapter 14 Expenses

Expenses consist of three major categories as shown in the diagram below.

There are direct expenses a business incurs for operating. These are wages of employees, supplies, office expenses, rent, electric and so on. The business would not operate without paying these expenses.

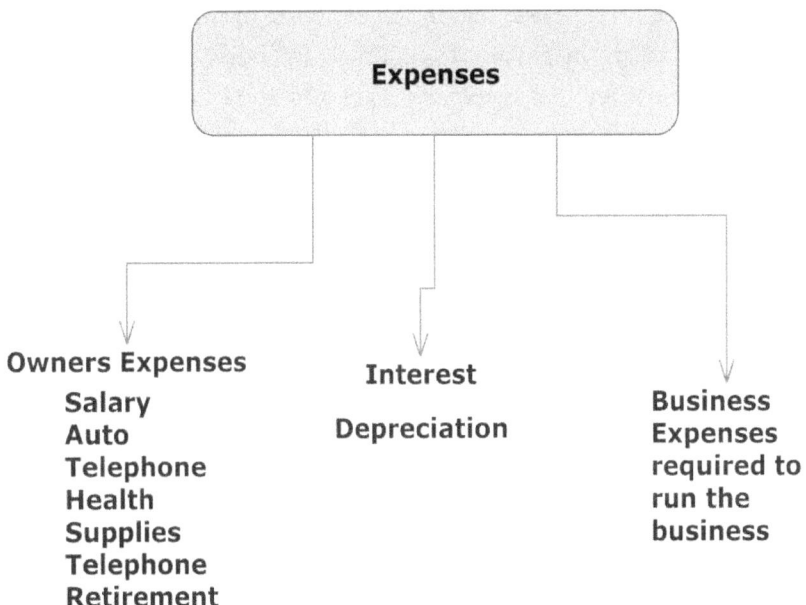

Then there is the interest expense. This expense is due to the owner financing, and is the cost of financing capital needed to operate or start the company. This could be a mortgage or interest on a loan from purchasing equipment. In selling a business all liabilities will typically be paid off so the interest expense is not relevant in estimating the value of the firm. The debt is paid off when the business is sold or refinanced by the new owner.

Depreciation is an accounting expense and does not impact the cash flow received by the owner. It reduces taxes but does not impact otherwise the amount of cash the owner will receive.

The owner's expenses are expenses that directly impact the income the owner receives. Embedded in these expenses are the owner's salary, automobile expense, telephone expense, health payment and supplies that are not necessary for running the business but are spent to benefit the owner. These expenses are added back to the net income to determine the amount of cash flow received by the owner. The owner will receive the sum of the net income plus the owner's expenses as his or her income.

Expenses can be either conforming or nonconforming. Conforming expenses will occur each year at the same relative level of expenditure. One can expect to have conforming expenses in the future that will either increase or decrease linearly with sales. A nonconforming expense is a onetime expense and is not expected to occur at that level again. For example, a fire in a kitchen of a restaurant would be a nonconforming expense. The buyer will not expect to see this expense.

An important part of valuation of the business is to analyze the expenses and categorize them into those required to run the business: those that are owner's benefits, and those that are nonconforming.

Chapter 15 Finding the True Profit

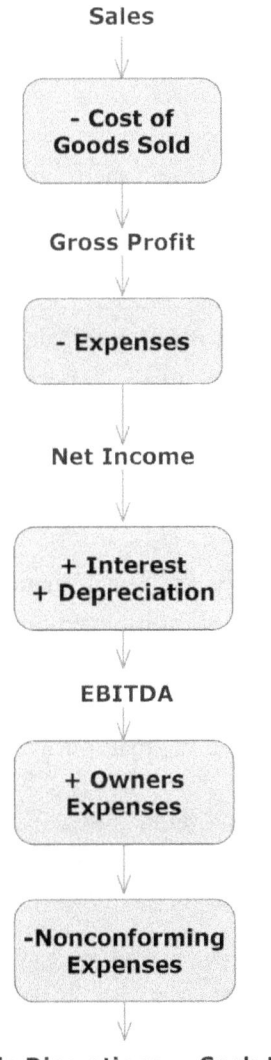

Sales

- Cost of Goods Sold

Gross Profit

- Expenses

Net Income

+ Interest
+ Depreciation

EBITDA

+ Owners Expenses

-Nonconforming Expenses

Seller's Discretionary Cash Flow

The process of reconciliation consists of taking the basic financial statement and reconciling it to determine the true cash flow profit made by the owner that what we have labeled as Seller's Discretionary Cash Flow (SDCF).

It can be thought of as a three-step process. Step one is to add to the Net Income the interest and depreciation which are expenses that do not impact the money the new owner will receive. The result of this step is called EBITDA (Earnings before interest, taxes and depreciation). This is a well-known financial measure and is used to evaluate businesses.

The second step is to add the owner's expenses back to EBITDA. The result is the Seller's Discretionary Cash Flow. It is sometimes referred to as the adjusted EBITDA since EBITDA is adjusted to reflect the owner's personal expenses.

A third step is to adjust the profit for nonconforming expenses. This can be an adjustment made directly to an expense of its normal expected value or, for example, can be an adjustment to the rent paid by the business to reflect true market rent.

To obtain the measure of profitability of a business the financial statement must be reconciled to obtain the true profit in such a way that it can be compared to the profits of other businesses.

So reconciliation is a quest to find the real profit. Buyers ask, "Why should I buy, if I am not going to make real profit?" To perform reconciliation, it sometimes requires forensic accounting of the financial records to identify those expenses that should be reconciled to determine the true profit.

Then what is the real profit? The real profit is the SDCF or the profit seen by the owner adjusted by market rent and nonrecurring expenses.

Examples of expenses that are typically found in small businesses that require adjustments are the following:

- Family on the payroll that are not really needed, or that are overpaid.
- Office and Supplies that are used for personal reasons.
- Paying for other real estate not necessary for the business.
- Owner's compensation via charge card expenses which are not necessarily needed for the business.
- Vehicle expenses paid by the company, but which are personal.

- Vacations taken by the owner and charged to the company.
- Uniforms costs charged, but for personal use.
- Personal Medical Insurance for the owner.
- Adjusting Rent, if the seller was not paying the market rent rate.

In reconciling expenses, we introduce the concept of "add backs." An add back means taking an expense that is really compensation to the owner and adding the expense back to profit. It is an adjustment to the financials.

It is important that all these add backs be identifiable in the accounting system so that a buyer can identify and verify these reconciled expenses upon due diligence of the company. All add backs have to be traceable in the accounting system.

Many times a seller will own property and pay themselves rent. This rent payment may exceed the normal rent that the overall rental market is paying or it may be less than market rates. In either case an adjustment to expenses must be performed to the market rate.

As a buyer valuing the business one must make an adjustment to reflect the rent that will be charged by the seller, if the seller is leasing the property to you and is charging the same amount of rent that has been charged to the business.

Chapter 16 Valuation

To obtain the value of a business one must compare the business with others that are similar and that have been sold. This is the basic concept in Business Valuation.

In the previous chapters we computed the before tax adjusted profit due to the owner (SDCF). These results will be used to estimate the value of the business and the compare to other businesses.

This question is "how do we compare the profitability of this company to other business and obtain a value for it?"

The answer is that we use large historical data bases of sold businesses that are organized by business type that is known as the SIC code or Standard Industry Classification. These transactions have been accumulated for years. Data for typical business types have been recorded with the price for which each business was In addition the sales income of the business and what the profit has been recorded.

These databases are available for a fee to the general public. The data contains the following for each sold transaction.

Chapters 50 and 51 provide the statistics summary for various business types and their SIC codes. You can look up typical averages and high and low ranges.

The definition of this data includes.

- Selling Price.
- Seller's Discretionary Cash Flow (SDCF)
- Ratio or multiple which is Selling Price/SDCF.
- SIC or NAISC code which is business type.

The NAISC code stands for Northern American Industry Classification and it is simply another means to classify the business type.

Typical multiples of selling price to SDCF range from 1 to 3 for small businesses, but for larger businesses and selected business types, the range can vary up to 5 or 6. Conceptually the valuation process is shown below.

Seller's Discretionary Cash Flow (SDCF)

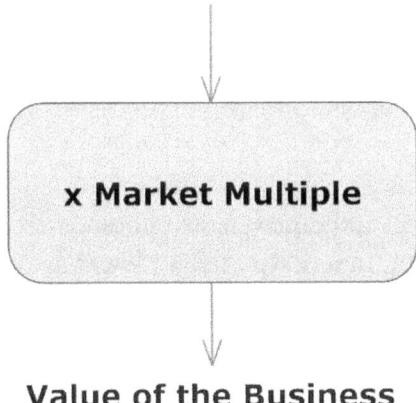

x Market Multiple

Value of the Business

The equation used to compute value is:

Value = Selected Multiple x SDCF

Generally, there are numerous transactions in the databases for a particular SIC code. When performing a valuation, one will select from these transactions or choose a multiple based on the statistics of the sample. If the business deserves a high quality rating with little risk and is growing, then we would select a multiple in the higher range of the transactions. On the other hand, if the company is weak in growth and there is significant risk, one might choose a multiple in the lower range.

For example, for restaurants the multiples let's say range from 1 to 3 and the average is 2.4. If the company deserves a high rating, you might select a multiple between 2.4 and 3 in the higher range, but if the company has a lower rating then the selected multiple would be less than 2.4. You must use your judgement when selecting the correct valuation multiple. You must assess if the business you are valuing has great performance with high potential or if it is average or if it is less than average.

Remember, that multiples in the databases assume a before tax cash flow incorporating the owner's salary and benefits.

There are also data bases available that are specifically for larger companies that contain additional statistics based on Net Income, EBITDA and Seller's Discretionary Cash Flow. For these larger companies the Seller's Discretionary Cash Flow may not be relevant. These valuations will be based on EBITDA. Multiples for larger companies can range to well over 5 to 6 or even higher in some instances.

A sample valuation worksheet is shown below for a particular business type and SIC code.

No	Annual Gross	SDCF	Sale Price	Sale Price To SDCF
1	1,881	377	395	1.048
2	226	88	100	1.136
3	226	88	100	1.136
4	387	55	65	1.182
5	367	108	150	1.389
6	226	61	85	1.393
7	384	120	180	1.5
8	937	100	158	1.58
9	696	384	637	1.659
10	469	123	249	2.024
11	469	123	$249	2.024
12	1,576	201	450	2.239
13	211	125	280	2.24
14	393	115	260	2.261
15	2,389	659	1,500	2.276
16	333	273	650	2.381
17	350	145	350	2.414
18	2,799	550	1,445	2.627
19	778	280	750	2.679
20	2,005	197	560	2.843
21	1,200	340	1,018	2.994
22	1,025	83	315	3.795

These are multiples for each of the 22 transactions of different sold businesses. Shown in the last column is the multiple or Sale Price to SDCF. This data is shown in dollars. The sales and the SDCF of each transaction are also shown. The columns are sorted by the lowest multiple to the highest and table is segmented into four parts each representing a quartile. If the business that you are valuing is a great business, then select a multiple from the highest quartile with multiples ranging from 2.627 to 3.795. But, if you believe the business is just average, then you might select the median value of the multiples which is 2.13. Let's say you have decided to use the median and the cash flow (SDCF) of the company is $100,000. The value is computed as:

Value = 2.13 x $100,000 = 213,000.

You, as the valuator, must make a decision as to the quality of the business compared to others in the market. One way to make a judgement of the quality of the business is to review the financial ratios. These ratios give insight on how well the business has performed over a specified time period. The higher your quality rating, then the higher the comparable should be.

Chapter 17 For what price shall I sell it for?

The value the business has been determined and proposed selling price has been established. Then the question is "for what price should the business be advertised for?"

Ultimately it boils down to what the seller perceives that he or she needs out of the sale, and for what the seller thinks it will sell for. The financial analysis and valuation has been done and now it is up to you and the seller to assign an advertised price. If there is no one in the market who will buy at this price, then it won't be sold no matter what the valuation says. You will find this out once you have the business on the market.

Some sellers look at the valuation, and then look at their retirement or other financial needs that may be urging them to sell. Some may think that they can sell it for less than the valuation to insure it will sell to insure they can retire. Some may price the business higher to leave room for negotiations.

Many times there is very little market data available to guide the seller as to what the multiple or price should be. Then it comes back to the seller to determine an acceptable price. If it is a highly desirable business, with a lot of potential, then a high multiple might be required even though there is no market data. It may be a unique business.

If it is a common business type, where many exist and have been sold, then it is better use the market data to determine the price. Ultimately, it is the Seller's decision to set price. Set it at the Seller's desired price and let it go to market. You will find out if it is a saleable price with what the market does in response.

If you have done your homework, your financial analysis, your valuation and price decision analysis, then you will have done your best. Don't worry about underpricing or over pricing, you will find out from the market.

Remember, there is a lot of time between listing it on the market and actually selling or closing on a business. It is not sold until the closing is done and the keys have been turned over to a buyer.

Chapter 18 How much do I get when I sell?

When the business is sold the seller will be taxed by the Federal Government in three ways. It will be taxed on the Capital Gain, depreciation recapture and income from earnings

Gain before Tax = Sale Price – Selling Expenses.

Taxable Capital Gain = Gain before tax – Original Investment.

Capital Gain tax = 20% x Taxable Capital Gain.

Depreciation Recapture Tax = 25% x Accumulated Depreciation.

Business Income = Accounts Receivable – Accounts Payable.

Business Income Tax = Corporate Tax Rate x Business Income.

Total Tax = Capital Gain Tax + Deprecation Recapture Tax + Corporate Income Tax.

Proceeds from Sale = Gain before tax + Business Income – Total Tax.

If the business is kept the business more than one year then the seller will pay based on a long term capital gain tax rate. The long term tax is smaller than the normal corporate tax rate. If the seller has owned the business less than one year, you will pay a short term gain at the tax rate of the corporation as the capital gain tax rate.

If equipment has been depreciated the seller will be taxed on depreciation recapture rate of 25% of the amount claimed as depreciation.

If, as part of the agreement to sell the business, the seller will receive the receivables then this money will be taxed at the normal corporate rate. If the seller is also responsible for paying the accounts payable, the taxable income will be the amount of the receivables less the payables.

In computing the capital gain the seller can subtract your selling costs. These may include fees from attorneys, accountants and brokerage commissions. Once these expenses are subtracted the basis or original investment can also be subtracted from the capital gain. The basis includes costs you have incurred purchasing the company originally, or investing initially, as well as the value of any assets you purchased after depreciation.

The resulting gain, after the selling costs and basis is subtracted, is called the capital gain. The capital gain tax applied to the gain will determine the tax owed from the gain you made on selling the company. In the past this tax has varied from 15% to 20%. As of the publish date of this book the tax is 20%.

The seller must add the depreciation recapture tax to determine the total tax owed.

The net you will receive is the sale price less selling costs, less the tax owed.

There is another factor that may come into play in determining your proceeds which is the deal structure. If in the deal structure there is part of the sale price allocated to a non-compete agreement, then the seller has agreed to a hidden tax. A non-compete agreement is taxed at the normal income tax rate, rather than the capital gain tax rate. Depending on the deal, this can represent a huge amount of tax burden that the seller would not have to pay if the sale price was totally allocated to the sale of the business. Sellers should not agree to put part of the price on this agreement.

Of course the buyer will have some tax advantages and legal advantages if a significant amount of money is allocated to a non-compete agreement.

Also, you may be taxed by your state government depending in which state you live. Check with your accountant.

Chapter 19 How much do I need to buy the company?

How much do I need to purchase a company?

The buyer will not just need the sale price to fund acquisition. The buyer will need enough to cover the following:

- Sale Price.
- Inventory Cost.
- Working Capital.
- Fees and costs associated with sale: attorneys, accountant

Inventory is usually over and above the sale price of the business, and must be paid at closing. The main reason is that inventory fluctuates each day of operation of the business. The price of the inventory is the cost for which the seller purchased it.

Working capital must be sufficient to cover the operation of the business for several months until the cash flow from receivables is stable and recurring under new ownership. This time period might be for 30 to 60 days and is the difference between the receivables and payables at the time of closing. The amount needed may differ if the business has seasonal sales patterns.

If the property is being sold then the buyer will need the down payment and closing costs on a mortgage. If property is being leased then the buyer will have to pay first and last month's rent plus a deposit.

Chapter 20 Marketing and Advertising Plan

There must be a plan to define how you are going to reach out to and communicate with buyers. The good news is that you have the internet to help us. Today it is the single most powerful tool we have for selling a business. You must take advantage of it.

The other good news is, that if it is a profitable business, there are many buyers seeking your business. There will always be buyers who are looking for a good investment. It is a worldwide marketplace; buyers will respond from all over the world and investors always will seek good investments.

You can also advertise in newspapers, trade journals, magazines or even the Wall Street Journal, but remember that the internet is the single most powerful vehicle in existence and is the most cost effective.

If it is a small business, such as a restaurant or a retail shop, you can effectively advertise in a local newspaper in addition to the internet.

If it is a specialized, technical, construction business or a retail business carrying special products then trade journals can be a effective method of advertising.

For medium to larger businesses, the Wall Street Journal can provide the buyers who may have the capability to purchase a medium to large company.

For advertising in local newspapers, you will provide your telephone number and/or your email address. For magazines or the Wall Street

Journal, you can provide the same as your contact information. Just make sure your contact information does not breach confidentiality.

For the internet the following websites provide good exposure for advertising.

www.BizQuest.Com

www.BizBuySell.com

Many others may be used. Just Google "business for sale."

You must provide the critical set of data that a buyer will want to see. It should be designed to attract attention. Headings should be "eye catching." Examples: "Growing Business," or "High Profits, High Growth." Describe what the business does and why it would be a great investment. It is your chance to grab the buyer's attention.

Each business will be given a classification or separated in a category. Make sure the business is located in the correct category, so when the buyer searches the listings for a business type, the website will display your business. If this is not done properly, the right buyer may never see your advertisement.

Include gross sales, cash flow, profit or seller's cash flow. Also document assets that come with it such as furniture, fixtures and equipment inventory.

Real estate, (included or not) as well as "lease or purchase" should be advertised. Include your email address and telephone number where the buyer can contact you.

Advertising is like fishing. The more bait and the more lines in the water, the more bites you are going to get. If you really want to sell your company use plenty of bait. Put many lines in the water and hopefully catch more fish. Be bold. Be confident. Envision yourself selling your company. You can do it.

Chapter 21 Dealing with Buyers

There is always a buyer somewhere. Have patience and wait for the proper opportunity, then size up the buyer.

Is it an investor looking for a long term investment that has a plan and vision to build the business? Is it someone who gets things done and is a decision maker; not afraid of risk? Does the buyer know something about the business? Sometimes, having a buyer that is knowledgeable about the businesses is not required, especially if the buyer is a fast learner, open minded and easy with whom to work.

Is it better to deal with a bad buyer versus none at all? The answer is no. It is always better to keep it on the market and find the right buyer. Don't waste your time on a bad buyer. It may take more time to get a good prospect, but as long as you have evaluated and priced the business correctly, a good buyer will come.

Many transactions will require holding paper, if for no other reason than the buyer believes he needs to keep the seller on the hook. And then again, sometimes there are no other financing alternatives available. For the seller the key is to get most of the money at the time of closing and minimize the amount of paper the seller must hold. Remember, the seller must be willing to take back the business if the buyer fails to pay the note.

Good buyers are ones that know the business and are cash buyers, ready and willing to buy.

Even though you may be dealing with multiple buyers, only one buyer will purchase the business. It is difficult, if not impossible, to bid one buyer against another. Treat each one individually. Many times buyers will pull out of negotiations if they know they are bidding against other buyers.

How do you motivate a buyer to make an offer? First, remember that you are always trying to sell and that you should never say anything bad about the business. A big part of your motivational power is your positive attitude.

You must educate the buyer.

You must establish trust with the buyer. This may take time but ultimately it is the reason businesses get sold.

When negotiating with a buyer, it is not *what* you say many times, but *how* you say it. Remember, everything is negotiable.

You have followed the advice in selling your company. You have advertised the critical information enough to entice buyers to seek more information. If it is an internet inquiry, you will get an email giving the buyer's name, email, telephone number, address or location. They will be seeking more information. If you have advertised in the newspaper or magazine, then you will get either a call or an email inquiry.

You have the inquiry. What next?

Golden Rule - If it is a business sale that you want to keep confidential, then do not give any information without having the buyer sign a Nondisclosure confidentiality agreement (NDA) and a buyer's qualification form.

If it is an inquiry from the newspaper or a magazine, always take down the buyer's contact information and email. Then send them a summary of the offering, similar to that provided on your internet advertisement. You may have to provide some basic information on the phone.

There are those buyers who will call and try to get all the information on the phone without signing a nondisclosure agreement. Don't fall for it! No matter how friendly they are, or how friendly you are. Always have your communication in writing. It is specific and you can keep track of it.

Take their information down, including their email address, and email them an NDA and a buyer's qualification form with instructions for faxing or emailing these completed forms back to you.

The buyer's qualification form will have a request for the buyer to copy their driver's license and fax it as part of the buyer qualification. If it is an individual buyer, then this request will insure that the buyer is who he or she says they are. If it is a company that is responding, then you should request the company's website or company information.

Once you have received a signed NDA and Buyer Profile Information you must review it. If you do not think the buyer is qualified or you are uncertain about the buyer's intentions, then do not send the information. You can tell them that they do not have enough financial resources to purchase the company or you can simply ask for more information. Remember the buyer may be asking the seller to finance part of the acquisition; you must get the right buyer whom you can trust and is capable.

Warning! There are those out there on the internet that are fictitious. Con artists! There are also people that are not smart enough to know they do not have the ability to buy your business and run it properly, or they may be just tire kickers! Your job is to stay clear of these people. They will waste your time and make your life difficult. Why send them your confidential information? A con artist can ruin you and your seller's life and business. Please take heed!

Keep it all in writing!

Once you have an NDA, then email or fax the memorandum, and wait for their response. They will no doubt email you more questions. Answer all questions in writing as quickly as you can. Do it with emails. Keep track of what you have said and what is being asked. Sometimes, from a buyer's inquires, you can learn that you have to update your confidential memorandum.

A good buyer continues to inquire with more questions.

If a prospective buyer continues to ask questions and you have assessed that they have good intentions, then you will move to the next step in the acquisition process. You will need more detailed information about the buyer, or via internet, perform searches to verify the buyer's information. You really want to know who this buyer is. Is he or she truly qualified, and is it feasible to work a deal with him or her?

You will need to evaluate your buyer in more detail. When interviewing the buyer these points are really important.

- Listen.
- Answer all questions as soon as you can. Keep the momentum moving.
- Over time attempt to gain the buyer's trust.
- Put everything in writing so you can track what has been said.
- Never say a bad word about the business.
- Try to stay in control.

Once a good buyer is identified and their questions have been answered in writing, the buyer is ready obviously ready to move to the next step. Now there are several options:

Have a conference call with the buyer and seller to discuss how the business operates. You can arrange a visit to the business with a face to face meeting, or you can solicit a nonbinding offer or letter of interest.

If there is a visit to the business, then it should be arranged after hours of operation.

The objective at this stage of acquisition is to provide the buyer enough information to allow them to make a nonbinding offer.

You want to ask the buyer if he or she needs anything else before making an offer. Your goal is to solicit an offer.

The message to the buyer is that you have stated your offering and now it is up to the buyer to respond. You can tell them that the offering is firm, or you may say that you are always open to all offers. But keep in mind your objective is to solicit an offer.

You might say that there are others interested in the business. However, watch out! For some buyers this strategy may "backfire", and some do not want to become part of what they may perceive as a bidding war. Sometimes it is not wise to pit one buyer against another. Many buyers will lose interest if they believe that there are others aggressively pursuing the business, but at the same time it may be worth warning the buyer that there are others interested in the business. It pays to be careful.

The result that you are looking is to have the buyer propose a nonbinding offer. It can be a binding offer with contingencies. It is almost always better to seek a nonbinding offer first from the buyer in order to insure that there is a meeting of the minds between buyer and seller before moving to the next step. Once the buyer has submitted the offer and you can counter. You can say that their offer is not in the "ballpark," or you can say it is acceptable. If the offer is accepted then the next step, which is evaluating a detailed proposal from the buyer. Detailed negotiations may now occur.

The question is "how sophisticated is your buyer? Is he or she an investor? Are you dealing with a public company? What techniques will the buyer use to evaluate your company?"

You should understand the buyer. This will serve you well in reaching a successful negotiation of a deal.

Chapter 22 Private Equity Buyers

Some may say that if you have a Private Equity Group (PEG) interested in your company, then you will be led down the path of milk and honey and will up end up rich!

Believe me when I say that this is not the case. Selling to a PEG may be the most difficult path to take and is a path riddled with pitfalls and risks. In some cases, it is worth trying, but you should keep your options open.

Private Equity is simply a group of investors who are working together to pool their money in order to make investments in real estate or businesses. Their only interest is how the business will perform financially and what financial risk they may be taking.

If you have a medium to large size company, then Private Equity Buyers and Investors may be interested in purchasing your company.

You should understand the motivations of a PEG.

- To make a yearly return on their investment is their main objective.
- They eventually to sell the business at a profit.
- They want to combine your company with others for economies of scale to increase profit.
- They want to take your company public along with others to increase their wealth.
- Their acquisition strategy is generally to limit their cash outlay. They want the owner to stay on and take an equity

stake in the company, or to have a seller's note and use other sources of financial leverage to perform the acquisition.

The level of difficulty selling to a Private Equity Group is high. Many times they require audited or reviewed financials. They will typically require that the owner stay on and operate the company for several years. They want a certain level of working capital left in the company, even though they may be purchasing your company as an asset purchase. If you agree to leave working capital in the business, then the overall sales price you will receive is effectively reduced by this working capital amount.

In an asset sale, the seller retains the accounts receivable minus the accounts payable. This can be a substantial amount of money in most cases. In Private Equity deals that require leaving working capital in the company, the seller receives less amounts. The seller can negotiate a higher sales price to cover this working capital amount.

A Private Equity group may require the seller to help them raise capital which they can use to buy your company. There may be presentations to investors in the Equity Group that are required. The seller would be raising the capital to buy their own company. This is not fair.

When will a Private Equity may be good alternative? When they can merge the company with other companies they already own or are in the process of buying. The combination of several companies may enhance the value of each, and of course the value you may receive for your company. But even so, PEGs are very good negotiators. Watch out!

Traversing a Private Equity acquisition is no doubt a difficult task, and for some it may be the only way to sell their companies. In many cases it may not be worth it if other buyers are available.

Chapter 23 Showing Your Business

During the acquisition process, the buyer will ask to meet the seller or to tour the facility and possibly meet your key employees. It can be a critical step in selling your company. The seller may have to do this in order to sell the business.

First and foremost, remember the business is being sold not the seller – the seller won't come with the business necessarily. At the same time the buyer must believe the seller will be easy to work during the acquisition and transition process. You are selling the business first and foremost without the seller being part of it.

Be honest, straightforward and informal. The buyer wants to hear that the company is easy to run, and that the business environment contains a great opportunity for growth.

Keep everything confidential. Make sure the buyer understands this .There will be a time and place to communicate to employees about the acquisition, and in the early stages of the acquisition process it is not the time.

Chapter 24 Negotiation

Golden Rule- You are the salesman. Treat the buyer as a customer. He or she is your friend. He or she may be the one who allows the seller to retire, to play golf and to travel. He or she is not the enemy; you have to negotiate a deal where both the seller and buyer are happy. "Selling mode" means always emphasizing the positive. You are a cheerleader for your business. Accentuate the positive and re-emphasize it to the buyer whenever you get a chance.

This rule logically leads us to another Golden Rule.

Golden Rule - Perception is everything. It is what people perceive that makes them buy. It can be real or not. Portions of it may be real or not. Many buyers perceive the life style that they can live owning a business. That is what drives them to purchase. You can only strengthen that perception by providing facts and figures with a positive selling attitude.

While you are negotiating, there are other important considerations.

Valuation and cash flow are the numbers that are important and cannot be overlooked. This is why businesses are sold. Is the buyer paying what the business is worth? Do you really have it priced correctly? What kind of proceeds will the seller get from the deal structure?

Keep these important points in mind during negotiations.

Assessment of risk is critical.

- You need to ask yourself "Can I make it to the closing table with this buyer?"
- What does the deal structure look like in cold hard cash flow to me and for the buyer?
- Can the seller achieve their goals from the proceeds the seller is getting from this company?

Here is some other advice you should consider during negotiations.

Never negotiate face to face, always do it in writing via email. Unless you are a professional negotiator, you will most always fail in face to face negotiations. This is also true for both buyers and sellers, simply because one on one negotiations become too personal, and each party will not have the time to make objective assessments and decisions.

It is also important to remember that you only need one buyer. No matter how tough the negotiations are, the buyer is your friend. Treat him as such.

In this step of the overall process you have communicated to the buyer that his or her offer is acceptable and you want to move to the next step.

Chapter 25 Deal Structure

You have a serious offer. Now what?

The offer is in the ballpark of acceptability. This means you know the business can be sold to this buyer. The process now moves into a negotiation stage.

Some buyers who feel confident enough now will submit a Letter of Intent or Purchase Contract to "cement the deal." This is the documentation you need to get the deal done, since it is a concrete offer in writing.

The offer will have a structure; we call this the "deal structure." You have stated what you were looking for as a deal in the confidential memorandum. At this point you have a current offer you have negotiated, or are in the process of negotiating.

The structure can have several components including:

- Down payment at closing.
- Seller note with time period and interest rate.
- Payment for non-compete agreement.
- Payment for receivables, payables, inventory and/or working capital.
- Earn out provisions.
- Stock in a new company – or keeping stock in your company.

An Earn Out is where the buyer pays the seller some of the proceeds, based on the future performance of the company.

If the stated performance is not achieved, the seller will not receive that payment that is specified in the Earn Out.

Many sellers will not consider an Earn Out option, especially if they are not planning to stay working in the business since they have no control over how the business is operated.

There are those situations where an Earn Out may work toward the seller's advantage. Maybe cash part of the payment is close to the value expected and the company is growing. Then the Earn Out could result in greater or higher proceeds than the expected value of the business. The seller would get more for the company with the Earn Out than without it. If the payout formula is stated that the seller can receive more money if the performance is exceeded. In this case Earn Out formula allows performance greater than expected.

If the seller is considering an Earn Out, don't put a cap on it's high limit. Only put a cap on the low side. For example, let's say the Earn Out is based on achieving a level of sales volume. It could be formulated as:

"The Seller shall receive an Earn Out as a percentage (say 5%) of sales volume over $1,000,000 with no upper limit. "

Some Earn Outs are based on profitability. In this example it is based on sales and really has no upper limit on payout. If the sales are less than $1,000,000, of course the seller will not receive any Earn Out according to the formula.

In either case of a seller note or Earn Out, you should structure the deal where most of the value for the business is paid at closing not dependent on an Earn Out. Let's say the selling price is $1,000,000, then the seller might agree to an Earn Out of $100,000 and receive $900,000 at closing. You will then have received most of the value you expected at closing and the Earn Out makes sense.

In terms of a Seller Note one strategy is to require external collateral such as real estate or some other tangible asset that could be liquidated. Many times, sellers force a buyer to seek other financing alternatives such as a small business loans though the Small Business Administration (SBA) by requiring external collateral or cash.

A promissory note, or seller note, is a promise to pay the seller from the buyer. It contains:

- When the payment is to be made.
- The amount of the payment.
- Interest charged on the note.
- What happens if the payment is not paid?

It is legally binding. The seller can sue the buyer and get a judgement. The seller will retain a security interest on the property or assets of the business that is sold. Many times the agreements contain clauses that legal fees must be paid by the buyer if the seller has to sue for payment. These agreements also contain clauses such as an acceleration clause where if the buyer does not pay in so many days, then the total note is due in full.

There are legal protections that can be built into the deal if the buyer fails to pay. Some of these are:

- Have the promissory note co-signed by the buyer's spouse or guaranteed by another party.
- Have a second mortgage on real estate owned by the buyer.
- Have a security agreement with buyer to take back the business assets if payments are not made
- If the business operates in rental space, seek the right to take back the lease.

Negotiating the non-compete agreement in the deal structure is extremely important unless the seller absolutely knows he or she will never be a future competitor. Limitations that a seller may want to include in a non-compete agreement are:

- Limit and define precisely what types of activities you cannot perform.
- Specify activities the seller reserves to do after the sale of the company.
- Limit the agreement to the smallest geographic area as possible.
- Limit the time period from two to three years if possible.

Many sellers do not know that they can negotiate this agreement and should do so.

Make sure the seller is happy with all aspects of the deal structure and is the deal for which the seller was looking when you started the process. Make sure the seller is not an unnecessary risk in getting full payment for your company. It all comes down to having a good deal structure.

Chapter 26 LOI or Purchase Agreement

The Letter of Intent (LOI) or Purchase Agreement stage is next following the agreement to a deal structure. Now both the buyer and seller agree to work together and agree to the deal structure in writing. Signing a written agreement binds both buyer and seller into the task of working together toward a final contract and closing.

These agreements provide a written statement of:

- Seller price and deal structure agreement.
- What the deal includes or does not include.
- Provision for buyer due diligence; how long and under what conditions.
- A target closing date.
- Definitive plan to develop a final contract.
- Provision for a deposit on the business.
- Statement of confidentiality.
- Whether the business is allowed to continue to be marketed or not.
- Any contingencies in the purchase, such as the buyer having a contingency to get financing before the deal can close.

If a real estate purchase is part of the transaction, there can be contingencies on financing as well as conditions for an Environmental Phase 1 Study.

For many small businesses, the buyer and seller can sign a purchase agreement directly, with a provision that due diligence and other contingencies must be satisfied before closing on the sale. In this case there is no need to develop a final contract; the purchase contract is all that is needed.

In the case of either a letter of intent or purchase agreement one must understand about deposits. The buyer will provide a deposit on the business so the business will be taken off the market and not sold to another buyer. This deposit is generally held by a third party as an escrow. The theory with this deposit is that if the buyer backs out from buying the business, the seller will receive the deposit. Most of the time the conditions of the deposit are that the business must pass the due diligence tests and the buyer must obtain acceptable financing, or that the buyer and seller will successfully negotiate the terms of a purchase contact. Of course there may be terms and conditions in the contract which both the buyer and seller cannot agree upon and the deposit would then be returned to the buyer.

Realistically, the deposit is subject to many conditions and so is almost never "nonrefundable." It is only nonrefundable if the buyer backs out and all other conditional items have been satisfied.

Your advice to the seller – your objective it to sell your business not to collect a deposit!

The seller and buyer should always have an attorney review the LOI or Purchase Agreement. It almost always should be an attorney who has experience with commercial transactions, either for real estate or businesses. If you are serious about selling, you should also be careful not to allow your attorney to negotiate the terms of the deal structure or the deal itself. It will almost always "kill the deal." Attorneys are great in minimizing your legal risk and should focus on this. By definition, it is between the seller and buyer to deal with the business risk of selling your company. Let the attorney make the legal decisions and the seller make the business decisions.

There are those sellers who do not like to make decisions. Oftentimes, it is their wife, brother, brother-in-law or their lawyers who are part of making the decisions. The result is a buyer's nightmare. To be fair to buyers, let the buyer know early in the process who is the decision maker. They can then determine if it is worthwhile pursuing the acquisition at all. The best way to get the business sold is for the seller to make the decisions and not delegate them.

At this stage in the process of acquisition, due diligence, contract development and negotiations are performed simultaneously. The stress level can be high. Everyone's attention should be focused on getting it done. Once there is a signed purchase agreement, then the contract development and negotiation is complete.

Tired yet? Just remember what all the fun you will have when you sell your company and are retired.

Chapter 27 Due Diligence

You, the seller, should now be thinking about the end of the journey in selling your business. Many sellers start planning for the future; how they will invest; what they will do. These are about the things the seller should be thinking, because Due Diligence is one of the last big tasks. Almost always sellers begin to spend the money in their mind's eye. They m will need this vision of the future to continue.

You have advertised how your company performed and now it is time for the buyer to verify it. Once this is done, then the buyer knows that what you advertised is what he or she is going to get.

The buyer will verify financial data and other features of the business that have been advertised. This process is called Due Diligence. The buyer will need to have access to company records. He or she must be able to visit the site of the business, and in some cases, meet employees and managers. On most deals the buyer will be restricted from contacting customers. This is particularly important should the deal not reach the closing table.

Many times buyers are restricted from meeting some or all of the employees, until the later stage of Due Diligence or when it is complete and the buyer has made a deposit on the business.

The list below shows a typical Due Diligence request list. As you can see, it is very extensive and thorough. The buyer has the right to see everything at this point. Nothing should be held back.

- Sales Tax Returns
- Bank Statements
- Financial Reports from the Accountant- Including the General Ledger Payroll Reports
- Monthly Payroll registers
- Internally generated sales reports
- Federal Tax Returns – needed to verify financial statements
- County Tangible Tax Return
- List of Accounts with monthly sales volumes with description of payment terms
- List of Assets
- Contracts with customers, vendors, employees and equipment
- Accounts Receivable Aging
- Description of Real Estate sufficient to order appraisal and title search
- Information on Employee Benefits Plan, including health insurance plan
- List of Managers with current salaries and wages and length of employment
- List of Employees with salaries / wages and length of employment
- Service Records for vehicles and equipment
- Summary of Insurance Policies
- List of current suppliers
- Property Tax bills
- Utility Bills
- History of Property Maintenance Expenses
- Lease – review - can it be assumed? Can the new owner get one?
- Corporate Records – who owns the business
- Licenses and Permits required

One of the most important tasks for the buyer is to verify the cash flows reported in the offering. To do this he or she will review the financial records, including the general ledger, invoices, bank statements and other expense reports to reconstruct the cash flow as you have reported in the confidential memorandum.

The buyer will always perform legal Due Diligence to make sure there are no outstanding lawsuits or liens on the company or on the company's assets. The buyer must buy the company or the company's assets free of any encumbrances. Any issues must be resolved before a deal is done.

A parallel activity on many acquisitions is development and negotiation of a final contract. This typically occurs when there has been a letter of intent as opposed to a purchase contract. The letter of intent first defines the basic terms and the final contract expands it into a contract. Once the final contract is signed, then the next step is the closing, assuming that the buyer is satisfied with Due Diligence.

In most deals, either the buyer or seller can choose not to continue with the deal at any time. The buyer can always say that Due Diligence failed one of the contingencies were not met. The seller can also pull out for certain reasons, providing it is not to sell to another buyer who is offering a better deal. This could be possibly occur if that option had been written into the Letter of Intent.

At this point you should realize, more than ever, that you are still in the selling mode, and should be acting in this mode all the way until closing.

Chapter 28 Existing Contracts

Dealing with existing contracts almost always has to be dealt with during Due Diligence and after the contract is signed.

This is common for the lease on property and equipment. The Buyer must work with the seller and the landlord to draft a new lease for the buyer.

There are also contracts with customers doing business with the firm. These contracts must be reviewed to see if they are assignable. If not, then before closing you may have to work with customers to make sure their contract will be reassigned and will continue. Those customers who have done business with the firm will cooperate and reassign the contract or write a new one for the buyer. Business is business – it makes sense.

Most small businesses are doing business with their customers without formal written contracts. In these cases, the buyer will need to be convinced that these customers will stay.

There may be leases on cars, trucks, equipment, or property. These leases must be reviewed and dealt with before or at closing.

During this time period the question is "How shall you approach customers?" It is important that the seller can and should work with the buyer to contact customers. It has to be done carefully. Remember the business is not yet sold, and the buyer may not want to buy the business if he or she cannot get contracts reassigned, new contracts signed, or existing customers agreeing to stay on with "business as usual."

Generally, assumption of loans is not done. Debt is not reassigned or assumed, but this could be a negotiated as part of the deal structure. A new loan agreement may be drafted with the new owner being responsible. Of course a loan cannot be kept with the previous owner's name. This could be disastrous, should the new owner not pay.

Loans to owners are excused during acquisition. It is common to see such loans on balance sheet financial reports of small companies. Many times they are on the balance sheet and at closing, these loans are simply written off the books.

Chapter 29 Asset vs Stock Sale

When the buyer purchases the stock of the company, then he or she buys the all the assets and the total liabilities. This includes current liabilities and current assets. This means the buyer gets the working capital at the time of sale in a stock sale.

With an asset sale the buyer will buy the tangible assets and goodwill of the company. He or she does not buy any liabilities, either current or long term, and usually this does not include current assets such as cash and receivables. In an asset sale, the seller must designate whether or not any portion of the current assets come with the business. Sometimes it is negotiated but for the most part it goes to the seller.

The price of the business for a stock sale should typically be higher than for an asset sale assuming that long term liabilities would be excluded in the corresponding asset sale.

Stock Sale Price = Asset Sale Price + Current Assets – Current Liabilities + Long Term Liabilities.

In either case cash and marketable securities would not be included in a stock or asset sale.

Sometimes in an asset sale, buyers will try to negotiate that a sufficient amount of working capital be left in the company. As discussed above an asset sale working capital generally does not come with the business.

In this case the buyer will make an offer as in an asset sale and specify that a fixed amount of working capital (current assets – current liabilities) be included. This by definition is an offer that is lower than the asking price in a typical asset sale.

One of the reasons that sellers do not specify working capital to be included in the price is because the working capital changes day by day depending on the operational cash flow. For some companies this is hard to predict and changes throughout the year.

Many buyers will not make an offer to buy stock for legal reasons. Their attorneys will advise them that the company they are purchasing could have an unforeseen liability or legal action that the buyer will assume if he or she has purchases the stock. It may be difficult to find lawyer who will agree to advise you on a stock sale.

In in an asset sale the buyer will establish a new company and move the purchased assets into it. Because of this, purchasing the stock instead of assets can be very advantageous since the registration for assets and operational licensing associated with the business is already established and would have to be done again for a new company that would be established.

Experience has shown that in either case of stock or asset sale the purchase contract will cover unforeseen contingencies in indemnification clauses. It is the buyer's attorney that may drive the decision on which way to go - stock or asset sale. This is a personal perspective in risk of the buyer and the buyer's attorney.

Chapter 30 Preparation of the Contract

After you have signed a Letter of Intent, then at the same time as Due Diligence activities are performed, the buyer will present you with a proposed contract for sale with terms and conditions of the sale. This document is drafted by an attorney. You will have your attorney review and comment on it.

The contract should reflect the terms agreed to in the Letter of Intent. If it does not, then it should be rejected right away since this flows the "rules of the game." The business deal has been set in the Letter of Intent and now the legal words need to be wrapped around it to protect both buyer and seller.

The contract will also cover a number of other important agreements such as:

- Non-compete agreement.
- Employment agreement.
- Lease of Facilities or Purchase of Property agreement.
- Buyer Promissory Note.
- Stock Option agreement.
- Indemnification clauses.

Non-compete agreements are governed by state laws, so must conform to these laws or the agreement can be invalid. If the property is leased, most brokers have standard lease agreements that can be used. You should use a standard lease agreement rather than have anyone develop one from scratch. Likewise, it is better to use standard forms for sale of commercial property. However, the seller's attorney can and should review these agreements for a lease or property purchase.

The Stock Agreement would be used when the seller is to be awarded stock or stock options in the new company. If the new company or the buyer is a public company, there will be some limitations due to SEC rules on these transactions. It is important to get advice from an expert such as a stockbroker or any attorney experienced on stock transactions when stock is involved in the deal structure.

As discussed above, the purchase can be performed as a stock sale or an asset sale. You should have decided at the time of the Confidential Memorandum, or at least by the time you have a Letter of Intent, what you will accept or reject in terms of the type of sale.

If it is a C corporation, then the seller may save taxes from a stock sale versus an asset sale. Otherwise an asset sale or a stock sale should be acceptable. All this depends on your company, who owns the stock and what your company type is – a C Corporation, S Corporation or LLC.

If it is a stock sale, then the buyer buys all of the company stock. The buyer will own your liabilities, your receivables and your assets. If nothing is stated to the contrary in the purchase contract, they will also own any lawsuits your company has or may have in the future due to your past operations. Therefore if it is a stock sale, the terms and conditions must spell out what the buyer is receiving. If there is cash in the accounts, then the purchase price must be adjusted, if there are receivables that have been specified to be the seller's, then the purchase price must be adjusted.

The purchase contract will also have terms in it to indemnify the buyer from future lawsuits or liabilities that may arise in the future due to past actions of the seller.

In this same vein, the contract will contain a statement of warranty and representations designed to protect the buyer. As an example, if the seller states that he or she is selling a cow, then the seller warrants the buyer will get the cow, not just the milk coming out of it.

There are many attorneys who will not work on a stock sale, most are familiar with asset sales and will work only on these transactions. Of course, experienced transaction attorneys will work on either. Some attorneys do not like to deal with a stock sale situation because of having to litigate or specify the indemnification terms. Also, most attorneys will not do legal work for types of transactions where they are not qualified or have no experience.

An asset sale is conceptually simpler than a stock sale. The buyer purchases the company's assets including physical assets, goodwill customer base and all that goes with the business to make it a going concern. The buyer forms a new company or uses an existing company and generally renames the new company the name of the sold company. The sold company becomes a shell only.

In stock sale contract language, covering indemnification, warranty and representations are included and must be negotiated. The agreement may say that the buyer may not be sued directly due to the company's past operations, but the assets transferred could be subject to suit, so indemnification still must be addressed.

The asset sale suffers from the disadvantage that any contracts or leases, including customer contracts, must be assigned to the new company.

Experienced attorneys can navigate these issues. Those who do not have the experience may be very expensive, since you are paying for them to learn and they may not have the proper knowledge to guide you to a successful closing.

Remember, it is the seller's business deal and their company. Hopefully they have already asked themselves – "Do I really want to sell?" and the answer has been "Yes." They should not be influenced that it cannot be done. Hundreds of businesses are bought and sold every day.

Chapter 31 Real Estate

Real estate can be a benefit or it can be a dead weight in selling a business. The real estate value should be justified with sufficient cash flow from the business to cover real estate payment if it is to be purchased in the acquisition.

The problem may be that the selling price and the value of the real estate may not coincide with the profitability of the company.

As a seller you have the decision to lease or sell your property with the business. You can also lease the property with the option to purchase. Many sellers may not wish to lease their property to a new business owner for fear the new owner may bankrupt the business. The seller would then be left with an empty property.

In many cases, there may be no other options than to lease the property. The seller may have bought the property years ago when the value was low and now the property has grown in value more than the business. In this instance, selling the property is not feasible since it is too costly for the business to support mortgage payments. Therefore leasing at a lower market rate is the only option.

If the buyer chooses to finance the property through a bank, the bank will evaluate whether the cash flow of the business can support the mortgage. If it does not, the buyer would have to place a larger down payment to reduce the amount of the mortgage for approval of the loan.

There is the option of having seller financing for the sale of the property. The seller may require a significant down payment with higher terms than a bank. If the seller is financing, then he or she has to be comfortable with getting the property and business back if the buyer fails to pay. Seller financing on the real estate is conceptually less risky than on the business, since the real estate has tangible value on its own and may be sold without the business.

It is always recommended that a commercial appraisal of the real estate be performed before the business is listed. There are many firms that offer such services and the cost is relatively small. This has the advantage that both the buyer and seller will know the value of the property being offered. This appraisal document generally goes out with the listing information. However, if the buyer makes an offer and wants bank financing, the bank will require its own independent appraisal.

An environmental survey may be required for some properties. If the seller does not have one already then they may have to have one performed. The survey reviews environmental conditions such as the presence of gasoline tanks and will assess their impact, if any. If the seller already has a survey then that should normally suffice.

In some acquisitions the seller will have to specify what goes with the business and what goes with the real estate. This is particularly important for restaurants and the restaurant equipment. In may be a gray area for some businesses as to what property and equipment comes with the business.

The market rent for the property should be examined by the buyer in the buyer's valuation of the business. If the seller is paying above the market rent, then there is a built in profit and the profit should be increased and treated as an addback. But, if the rent is lower than the market rate then the rent needs to be increased and profits should therefore decrease. The buyer should also analyze the market rent to determine if the seller is offering to lease the property based on market rent. The buyer should try to negotiate the market rent of less.

As mentioned above, a commercial property appraisal will be necessary if the seller is selling the property. A commercial property appraisal consists of three methods of valuation of the property. It will compare this property to similar properties that have sold, and use this comparison to estimate value. It also uses an income approach to determine how much rent the property should generate, and then use that as a basis for valuation. Lastly, it will estimate value based on a square foot basis, using standards. In the end the three methods are factored together to come up with a single value.

Why is the commercial appraisal important? Because it defines the value up front in the negotiation process and takes the debate on property value off of the table. It is normally accepted as the price of the real estate by the buyer and does not have to be negotiated. If the appraisal does not meet expectations of the seller or buyer it can be a roadblock in selling a business. The property may have to be leased or the purchase price of the business will have to be negotiated.

Chapter 32 Purchase Agreement

As a seller you want to encourage the buyer to make an offer soon after you have supplied sufficient information for the buyer to do so. It is wise to ask first for a nonbinding letter of interest that provides the terms of purchase such as price, structure of the deal and timing.

If the letter of interest is a serious offer and is acceptable then you as the seller should ask the buyer for financial verification that he or she has the funds to purchase the business.

If there is a meeting of the minds then the next step will follow two alternative paths. The first path is a Letter of Intent (LOI) and the second is directly going to a purchase contract.

The LOI will bind the seller and buyer to work together until a contract is drafted and agreed to and due diligence is complete. It also may contain contingencies in it such as financing of the business and/or property. An example LOI is provided in Chapter 46.

The contract for purchase is similar to the LOI but contains much more details and contractual terms and conditions. It will contain and discuss due diligence requirements and may define contingencies before closing can be complete. This contract for purchase for a small business is generally a standard agreement that does not get customized too much for a particular transaction. It is a fill-in the blank document. For many small businesses it is the way to go since a new contract for purchase does not have to be developed and approved from scratch. A summary of the topics covered in the contract is provided in Chapter 47.

The seller may require the buyer put down a deposit of earnest money. Since there is still due diligence to be done and there may be contingencies this deposit can never be nonrefundable. Once the buyer and the seller sign the final contract at the end of due diligence and after the contingencies are met then the earnest money becomes nonrefundable.

There is always an issue at this stage as to whether to take the business off the market or leave it on while the final negotiations take place. The buyer does not want the seller to negotiate other offers and the Seller wants to continue to market the business in case the buyer backs out of the deal or they cannot reach agreement.

The structure of a deal contains many components as shown below.

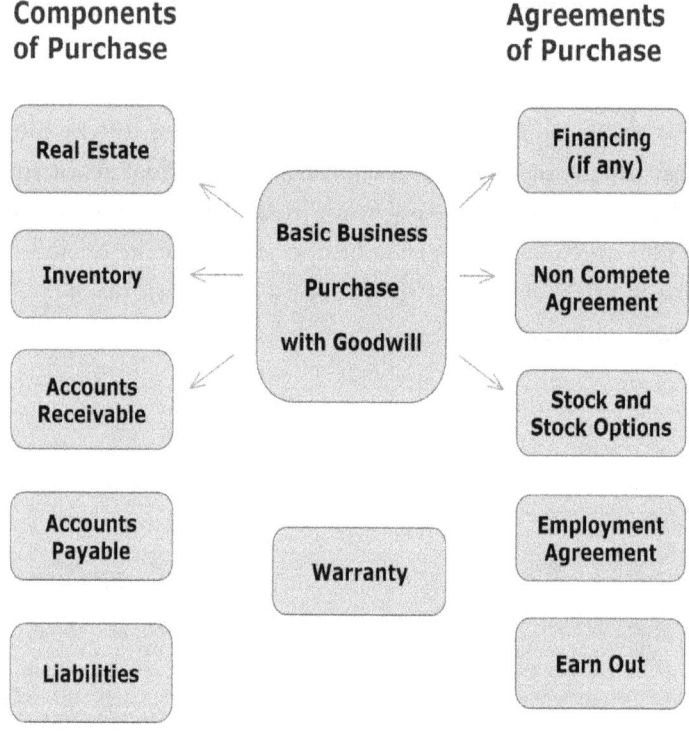

The purchase agreement will address each component to say what is included, what is excluded and how each component will be handled. It will address the various agreements that need to be made and agreed upon and what will happen after acquisition. Moreover, it will address the warranty as agreed to by the Seller. It is the single most important document in the acquisition.

Chapter 33 Closing Day

Finally, you are there. I bet you wondered if it could actually happen. It can and will. You deserve it and most sellers never regret it.

For the closing it is best to have a closing agent or attorney who does not represent you the seller or the buyer. The closing agent may be an escrow company or independent legal firm. Closing agents are experienced and cost effective. They have a staff dedicated and organized to handle such transactions. The second best option is to have your attorney perform the closing. Sometimes it is the buyer's attorney who will perform closing.

The closing documents should be provided to you and the buyer well before closing for review. In any case, there is another Golden Rule.

Golden Rule - Don't sign anything until the money has been wire transferred or a cashier's check has been deposited into the closing agent's escrow account. Everyone at the closing that is to sign the agreements must show their driver's license. The closing agent will verify the funds are there before closing can proceed.

Once you and the buyer sign the contract for purchase, it is the buyer's company not yours, you have no control. Make sure you are paid before anything is signed.

With an asset sale, there will be some work left to complete after closing. These are tasks that generally have to be performed after closing that include transfers of titles and registration for automobiles, trucks, contract assignments, telephone and utility transfers and the like. In terms of the receivables and payables there are several options:

- The net of the receivables and payables are paid at closing.
- Receivables would be paid to the Seller's bank account as they are received.
- Receivables paid in a lump sum 60 to 90 days after closing.

In any of these instances, some escrow may be held by the closing agent either for the buyer or seller until the receivable payments are complete.

Remember, at closing everyone's license must be examined to verify who is there and are they who they say they are.

Chapter 34 Working Capital

The buyer will need to know what the working capital requirements are. The buyer can ask the seller and many times they will have a good estimate.

In this section of the book working capital is discussed and methods of estimating it explained so you can estimate your needs for the company.

Working capital is an important metric for all businesses regardless of their size. It is a measure of a company's operating liquidity. Without sufficient working capital the business cannot pay for all of its short-term expenses and liabilities.

Working capital can also be described as the amount of money that a small business or start-up needs to stay in operation. Startups need to track their working capital because it is the amount of money they need to keep the business running until break-even and it starts earning a net profit.

Working capital specifically refers to the cash a business requires for day-to-day operations or for financing the conversion of raw materials into finished goods. Among the most important items of working capital are levels of inventory, accounts receivable and accounts payable.

Working capital of a company is defined by below as:

Working Capital = Accounts Receivable – Accounts Payable

There are several ways to estimate how much working capital is needed in a business.

Working Capital as a Percentage of Net Sales: Using this method the estimate the working capital requirement is based on the fact that the working capital for any firm is directly related to the sales volume of that firm. So the working capital requirement is expressed as a percentage of expected sales for a particular period. This approach is based on the assumption that higher the sales level, the greater would be the need for working capital. There are three steps involved in the estimation of working capital using this method.

- Estimate total current assets as a percentage of estimated net sales.
- Estimate current liabilities as a percentage of estimated net sales, and
- The difference between the two above is the net working capital as a percentage of net sales.

Working Capital as a Percentage of Total Assets or Fixed Assets: This approach of estimation of working capital requirement is based on the fact that the total assets of the firm consist of fixed assets and current assets. On the basis of past experience, a relationship between the total current assets and current liabilities and the total fixed assets or total assets of the firm is established. Using this approach the estimation of working capital depends upon the estimation of fixed capital which depends upon the capital budgeting decisions.

Both the above approaches to the estimation of working capital requirement are simple in approach but difficult to perform in practice.

Business Cycle: This approach is based on the overall business cycle of the firm and can be broken down as follows:

Compute the number of days for collection of receivables (NDR) from customers minus number of days of accounts payable (NDP) to suppliers. The difference equals Cash Conversion Period.

Cash Conversion Period = NDR – NDP

Assuming NDR = 98.9 and NDP = 54.9

Then the Cash Conversion Period = 98.9 – 54.9 = 44 days

The next step is to take the total estimated annual sales and express them in terms of sales per day. For example:

Assume the total sales were $18,252,533

Then the total annual sales of $18,252,533 / 365 days = $50,007 per day.

The number of days of sales to finance is the accounts receivable days minus the accounts payable days equals 44 days.

Cash Conversion Period = NDR – NDP = 44 days

Now take the number of days to finance, i.e. 44 days, times sales of

$50,000 per day for an estimated working capital requirement of $2,200,308. The formula for Working Capital is:

WC = Sales / Day * (NDR – NDP)

WC = 50,007 x (98.9 – 54.9)

WC = 50,007 x 44

WC = 2,200,308

The above example outlines the general steps involved in estimating working capital requirements using this Business Cycle methodology.

Chapter 35 C Corp vs S Corp or LLC

The C Corporation is the standard corporation, while the S corporation is a corporation that has elected a special tax status with the IRS. It gets its name because it is defined in Subchapter S of the Internal Revenue Code. To elect S corporation status when forming a corporation, Form 2553 must be filed with the IRS and all S corporation guidelines met.

Both corporations offer limited liability protection, so shareholders (owners) are not personally responsible for business debts and liabilities.

C corporations. C corporations are separately taxable entities. They file a corporate tax return (Form 1120) and pay taxes at the corporate level. Owners also face the possibility of double taxation if corporate income is distributed to business owners as dividends, which are considered personal income. Tax on corporate profit is paid first at the corporate level and again at the individual level on dividends.

S corporations. S corporations are pass-through tax entities. They file an informational federal return (Form 1120S), but no income tax is paid at the corporate level. The profits and losses of the business are instead "passed-through" the business and reported on the owners' personal tax returns. Any tax due is paid at the individual level by the owners.

Personal Income Taxes. With both types of corporations, personal income tax is due both on any salary drawn from the corporation and from any dividends received from the corporation.

The limited liability company (LLC) offers an alternative to corporations and partnerships by combining the corporate advantage of limited liability protection with the partnership advantage of pass-through taxation. With this tax status, the LLC's income is not taxed at the entity level; however, the LLC completes a partnership return if the LLC has more than one owner. The LLC's income or loss is passed through the LLC and reported on owners' individual tax returns. Tax is then paid at the individual level.

Double Taxation on C Corporation on the sale of the Company
If a corporation sells all its assets and distributes the proceeds to its shareholders in a liquidating distribution, the corporation is subject to tax on the asset sale and the shareholders are subject to tax on the distribution. The distribution of assets in liquidation is treated at the corporate level in the same way as if the assets were sold for cash and the proceeds distributed to shareholders in exchange for their shares. The shareholders would also have a tax on their gain measured by the difference between the liquidation proceeds (or the net fair market value of the assets if they are distributed in kind) and the basis of the shares in their hands. Thus, whether the C Corporation sells all of its assets and distributes the proceeds in liquidation or distributes all of its assets in liquidation, the tax consequences to the corporation and its shareholders are substantially the same. In both cases, there is double taxation. In general, the federal double-tax rate of 44.75% (plus applicable state tax net of any federal benefit from deducting state tax) should apply if the shares of the corporation are a long-term capital asset in the hands of the shareholders. In considering these alternatives, both corporate and shareholder tax attributes such as net operating or capital loss carryovers should be considered.

When you sell your business, the difference between being structured as an S corporation versus a C corporation can result in a multi-million dollar difference in your tax obligation. The advantages of being structured as an S corporation versus a C corporation are not readily apparent or completely clear-cut (we are talking U.S. tax code here after all); however, given the significant tax savings that can be achieved, it is worth taking the time to understand the advantages and disadvantages of both structures.

Asset Sale vs. Stock Sale
Double taxation for C corporations becomes a major consideration when you sell a company's assets. Most acquirers, especially those in the engineering and construction industry, favor asset sales over stock sales for a number of reasons. First, with an asset sale, acquirers are generally able to step-up the basis of the acquired assets, which results in a reduction of future taxes as acquired assets are depreciated at their new value. Second, asset sales allow buyers to select which assets they would like to acquire. Lastly, a buyer is able to specify the liabilities it is willing to assume with an asset sale; whereas, with a stock sale, the buyer runs the risk of assuming unknown or uncertain liabilities.

In an asset sale, a C corporation pays corporate taxes on the difference between the tax basis and sale price of the assets sold. Upon liquidation of the C corporation the owners are then subject to a capital gains tax on the difference between their cost or tax basis in the stock and the proceeds distributed from the liquidation.

An owner of an S corporation who is contemplating a sale does not face quite as great of a dilemma as an owner of a C corporation. Assuming there are no significant items of recapture or built-in gains (discussed below), owners of S corporations are generally indifferent to a stock or an asset sale from a tax perspective. This is because the profits of an S corporation are taxed as earned and the stock basis increases over time. Therefore, whether assets or stock are sold, owners of an S corporation generally only pay capital gains tax, at a current rate of 20%, on the amount over their basis.

Convert From C to S Corporation
There can be a striking tax difference between the sale of assets and sale of stock for a C corporation. Consequently, shareholders of C corporations strongly favor selling stock, rather than assets. However, as previously discussed, buyers strongly favor asset transactions, and, as a result, owners of C corporations are often forced to sell their business under less than optimal tax circumstances.

Consequently, it often makes sense for owners who are considering selling their business to convert from a C corporation to an S corporation in order to receive more favorable tax treatment upon sale, as well as to increase their basis every year their company makes a profit.

Consequences
Corporation sale of assets held by a newly converted S corporation can be treated as pass-through gains to shareholders. If assets previously held by the C corporation are sold during the 10-year

waiting period, a tax consequence based on the difference between the tax basis of the assets and their fair market value at the time of conversion is triggered.

You as a buyer or seller should be aware of the consequences of C versus S corporation tax consequences in selling or acquiring a business. Be sure to discuss these with your accountant.

Chapter 36 Special cases in Valuation

Intangible Assets - A business may own the rights to copyrights, patents, or trademarks even brand names. These assets are intangible and are intellectual property. If these assets are valuable to the market then they must be analyzed separately in the valuation of the overall company. The Seller will need a valuation specialist who is knowledgeable in valuation of these intangible assets. Once these assets are valued their individual values must be added to the overall valuation of the company.

There are those types of businesses where the potential for profit is so high and the future growth is so great that the selling multiple will be extremely high and can be in the 7 to 30 range. Businesses in the high technology or entertainment businesses could be in this classification. Be aware if your company fits into one of these categories. Your company and its assets may be more valuable than you think.

Accounting, Engineering, Civil, Surveying, and consulting firms require special consideration. These types of businesses are based on revenues where technical labor and services are sold. There may be no products. It is the people working in the company that are of value and how their services are demanded. Valuation and selling of these firms can be difficult and may be difficult to find a buyer. Sometimes it is a buyer in the same type of firm who wants to grow and expand or it may be another company of equal size that wants to merge. The synergies of both companies as one operation may weigh heavily on the acquisition.

Equipment Leasing businesses require special consideration in valuation. You must consider the physical depreciation and obsolescence of the equipment when valuing these firms. They will have fairly large depreciation expenses but a large part may be physical depreciation. In computing the EBITDA of the company all of the depreciation cannot be added back or it must be adjusted at the end of the reconciliation. You must consider the physical deterioration and replacement of equipment.

Minority and Control is an important consideration. The best way to describe this is to say it is when a percentage that is not a percentage. First of all, if there are minority owners (less than 50%) there must be an agreement with these minority owners to sell the business before the acquisition process begins. However, it may be possible depending on the bylaws of the organization that a stockholder may sell his or her shares unless there is an agreement not to with other stockholders. In any case if there are minority share owners then the valuation of those shares is technically difficult. There may be a case where the majority shareholder is buying out minority owners so that the company can be sold as one transaction. The value of the minority shares is not simply by taking the minority percentage say 20% and multiplying the 20% by the overall value of the firm. It will be less because the minority share will incur a minority discount. This means their value will be less than 20%. Thus the majority share owner will have a premium attached to their percentage ownership.

The reason is that the majority will have more control and other rights within the firm therefore their ownership comes with a premium sometimes referred to a control premium. Be aware of the minority discount for minority owners and control premiums for majority stockholders. It is the case where a percentage ownership is really not a percentage ownership but something less.

A synergistic purchase can be part of the equation. In some acquisitions a buyer has a built in profit or cost saving that will occur when their business purchases the business for sale. Combining the businesses is said to have a synergistic affect. The whole is greater than the parts. If you are selling the business to the general marketplace to any buyer without regard to the type of buyer then your valuation criteria is Fair Market Value. You should not consider the synergistic impacts of a potential buyer in valuation in the general marketplace.

Let's say you have a plastics company and you intend to sell your company to only another plastics company that is a larger firm. Then you can consider the synergistic impact of such a transaction in the price you are asking. Maybe your company will reduce the transportation expenses incurred by the large company in addition to increasing their sales and bottom line with your company's profitability. If you reduce the costs by $100,000 and the market multiple is three then the value of your company to the other has a built in $300,000 additional value. If you anticipate this type of sale you should consider these synergistic impacts as part of your negotiating strategy with the buyer.

Chapter 37 Special problem with Licenses

Some types of businesses have licensing requirements required by the State government where the business is located. New owners of the business would have to qualify for the license to own and operate the business. If the new owner already has the license this is not a problem. Otherwise the new owner will have to obtain a license. This may require testing or working for some time under a licensed employer to qualify.

To overcome this problem the old owner may stay on as an employee and become the qualifying licensee for the new company until the new owner has been qualified and obtains his or her own license.

Businesses that require licenses include electrical contractors, pool contractors, real estate companies, refrigeration and air conditioning, building contractors and plumbing companies.

Purchase contracts are often difficult to negotiate because the licensee's liability for work in the new company. The licensee would still be liable under state law even though he or she no longer owns the company.

There is always a work around plan to solve the problem. You may need to creative. There may be third party qualified licensee's that will assume a position in the company for compensation. The new company can use the third party until they have an employee who is fully licensed working in the company.

Chapter 38 Stock and Stock Options

Proceed with caution when stock options are on the table. There may be many pitfalls and you may end up with nothing. Maybe instead of options you could have simply negotiated a better price for the business instead with a cash deal.

There is no guarantee with stock options. You will not be receiving stock that you can sell for the price that you may have expected. You will have to write a guarantee into the agreement negotiate that the stock has a with a buyout guarantee with a minimum price. Realize that if it is small private company and you get stock as part of the deal you will be a minority owner. There may be no guarantees of income unless it is agreed to in writing as part of the contract for sale.

The other situation that occurs frequently is where a public company purchases a private company as part of a portfolio of businesses with the intention of improving their overall stock value and earnings. Sometimes companies are sometimes trading at small volume of trades and the stock share value is small compared to the rest of the market. You may be offered a large block of the public stock as part of the purchase. In this case you will need expert advice from a stockbroker or financial planner to evaluate the risk and earning potential of owning and then selling the stock. Typically there are restrictions on selling your shares.

You have the option to take a seller's note or cash instead of a stock deal. It is something to think about.

Chapter 39 Old vs New World of Brokering

 In years past business were bought and sold through by business brokers who were established in the local communities. This was done many times through newspaper advertising and direct mail. These brokers were maybe real estate salesman who had experience in business. Technology was not involved; only salesmanship.

Today brokering has changed dramatically. Business brokers are now certified and trained by national organizations and sales activity is done via the internet. The technology is quite sophisticated and the well trained broker can directly perform financial analysis and valuation as part of the tasks. To sell your business in today's market your broker must embrace technology and fully take advantage of it.

If you are going to use a broker to help you buy or sell a business use one that has been trained in business brokering and is certified by a national organization. Also, it is better to find a broker who has owned and sold their own business. He or she should have this firsthand knowledge from a seller's viewpoint. This will greatly improve your chances of getting your business sold.

Chapter 40 Asset Approach to Valuation

The asset approach is generally used for asset-intensive businesses, holding companies, and companies that are not generating adequate cash flow, i.e. companies that perhaps should be liquidated. This approach is usually not appropriate when appraising businesses with few assets, on-going businesses with large intangible assets, and service businesses and is generally not appropriate for appraising minority interests in a business. The asset-based approach is particularly appropriate when the ownership interest being appraised has the ability to liquidate or sell the underlying assets of the business.

The most common asset based method is the Adjusted Book Value Method. If warranted, one of several liquidation value methods may be used in this method.

The Adjusted Book Value Method consists of a review of every item on the balance sheet. Each item is reviewed to see if it needs to be adjusted to fair market value. Sometimes appraisals on individual assets must be obtained from real estate or machinery & equipment appraisers to accurately apply this method. The liquidation value method involves the review of either an orderly liquidation or a forced liquidation of all of the assets. In such cases, the costs of the liquidation must also be determined and accounted for. If the business is to be valued as an ongoing business, the liquidation method is not used.

Be aware of this valuation method even though it does not apply in selling an ongoing business and may not apply to your business.

Chapter 41 Income Approach to Valuation

The Income Approach to business valuation is presented here to be complete. You may see this method used if you have a medium to large size company. From a practical point only the larger companies use this method. Small business cannot be effectively valued using this method simply because the data is not available to accurately compute the needed cash flows and discount rate required by the financial models of the Income Approach. Most small to medium businesses are valued exclusively using the Market Approach.

In some respects if accurate data existed was available to you then the Income Approach could be judged superior to the Market Approach since it is based on the concept of the time value of money and company income rather than making comparison to other similar transactions using the Market Approach.

Before delving into the Income Approach one must understand the Time value of money for it is the basis of the Approach.

Take $100 today and invest it at 8% yearly interest. The investment would grow to be $215.89 in 10 years. One could say that $100 today is worth $215.89 in 10 years. This process is called compounding an investment made today into the future.

Or $215.89 in 10 years is worth only $100 today at 8% yearly interest discount rate. Realize if we have $100 in 10 years we would only have $46.32 today assuming a discount rate of 8%. This process is known as discounting the investment back to its value at the present time or year.

So having money today is worth more than in the future simply because you can invest it and compound it into the future.

The process of taking a future value and determining its present value at a specified compounding rate is called discounting the cash flow.

So money is said to have a time value because of the ability to grow it via compound interest.

Therefore a business that generates profit each year for the next ten years can be valued by discounting its cash flow using the concept of time value of money.

The task in valuation is to simply evaluate each of its cash flows and find out how much each would be worth today which is its present value. Once we do that then we will have the valuation for the business.

To perform this valuation we need to assume a compound interest rate we expect to make when we are investing as we assumed we could make 8% above. Once we discount each cash flow back to the present and then add each together we would then have the value of the business.

This method is called the Income Approach to valuation.

In some respects the Income Approach is the most rigorous but at the same time it is also the most difficult to use. First one needs the discount rate to determine the valuation. If you were investing in a bank savings plan or a bond this percent return or discount rate is known. It is what the bank or Bond Company would offer you. If you were making an investment in real estate, capital improvement project then this number is the rate of return you are looking for to actually make the investment be worthwhile to you and this number represents the return you are looking for on the investment.

In terms of business valuation we need the return the overall market needs and wants to buy the company since we are using the Fair Market Value as a valuation yardstick. We can only get this discount rate from statistics of the marketplace.

The best source of data for this is the comparable discount rate of a similar company that is public and trading in the stock market. This data is available from several sources. These sources accumulate stock market statistics. One source is the service provided by Ibbotson Associates.

The discount rate is the expected rate of return that a "typical" investor would require based on the level of risk associated with the investment. Discount rates reflect the risk associated with achieving the expected income from an investment.

Once a discount rate of a comparable company is found, we must adapt it to it to reflect the particular company that is being evaluated.

So a discount rate is the expected rate of return that a "typical" investor would require based on the level of risk associated with the investment. Discount rates by their nature reflect the risk associated with achieving the expected.

Using the stock market statistics the most common method used to determine the discount rate is called the build-up method. This build-up method computes a discount rate using the individual components of the return and adds them together to determine the total discount rate. Some of these components are available for publicly traded stocks as databases that are updated each year. Some of the terms are specified by the person performing the valuation and require judgment.

Using the build-up method, a discount rate is comprised of the following:

Discount Rate = Risk Free Rate + Equity Risk Premium + Industry Risk Premium + Size Premium +Company Specific Component

The Risk Free Rate and Equity Risk Premium is for the overall stock market for that year. The Industry Risk Premium is for a selected business type. The size premium is an overall premium depending on the size of the business you are studying and the Company Specific Risk Component is determine and assessed by the person performing the valuation for the business that is being valued.

Once we have the discount rate then we can compute the capitalization rate by the following.

Capitalization Rate = Discount Rate – Long Term Growth

The Long Term Growth is the growth rate that is expected company will experience in the long term which is typically 1% to 3%.

The higher the perceived risk of achieving the forecast income stream, the higher the discount rate. More formally, a discount rate is defined as a rate of return used to convert a series of future income amounts into their present value, where as a capitalization rate is a divisor (or multiplier) used to convert a defined stream of income to a present indicated value. Basically, the difference between the two rates is the capitalization rate equals the discount rate less the expected growth rate.

The discount rate that has resulted from the buildup method reflects the return on equity or stock value in the market place. In order to use the income approach using this rate we will need to discount a cash flow that reflects the value of equity for the business we are studying. Both the discount rate and the cash flow have to reflect this same basis and that is equity.

Therefore, the cash flow must be based on the change of equity that results due to the profitability of the firm. For this we need to compute the net cash flow to equity (NCFE) of the business for each year of valuation. The NCFE captures the impact of profit on the equity value of the business and that is why we use it.

NCFE = Adjusted EBITDA + Working Capital Changes + Capital Expenditures + Long Term Debt Changes

The Adjusted EBITDA is simply the seller's discretionary cash flow described in previous chapters and the other components are the changes that occur in the firm that either increase or decrease equity in the firm as recorded on the Balance Sheet.

With the NCFE for each year and the discount rate we can compute the present value of the cash flow to value the business.

Using this method of implementation the Income Approach can be used under two assumptions. The first is that the income cash flows will be equal over time called the single period capitalization and the second is that the cash flows are different each year of the valuation.

For single period capitalization of income the value is computed by assuming that it is the same each year of the valuation and is determined by the following equations.

Value = Cash Flow x (1 + growth rate) x Capitalization Rate

Where Cash Flow is the NCFE discussed above.

The Income Approach can get further complicated by analyzing the cash flows for each year into the future assuming that each year the cash flow is different and then evaluating the terminal value of selling the business at some future time.

$$\text{Value} = \Sigma_i \left(\text{NFCE}_i / (1+k)^i \right) + \text{NFCE}_n * (1+g) / \left((k-g)(1+k)^n \right)$$

Where i = 1 to n   g = yearly growth rate   k = discount rate

Σ_i is the summation of the term over i from 1 to n

n represents the last year of the valuation. The last term is called the terminal value of the firm and is the value of the firm at the last year of the valuation.

As we can see using the Income Approach for valuation of a small business is a difficult task and that is an understatement. One must make numerous assumptions and judgements to arrive at the right data to perform the analysis. The computation of the net cash flows to equity is difficult and determination of an accurate discount rate requires expertise. The risk of error using this approach for a small company is high in arriving at an accurate valuation compared to the Market Approach. Even so, this approach is based on evaluating the income generated by the company and the financial results on equity and so is used in numerous valuations particularly for large companies.

This approach to valuation probably does not fit your situation. It is presented here mainly to highlight the inherent difficulties in its implementation and to emphasize that overwhelmingly why the market approach is the most widely used method of business valuation.

Chapter 42 Excess Earnings Valuation

If you are selling your business as a result of a divorce then there is a high probability your business must be valued by the Excess Earnings Method by the court. It is the most accepted method used by the courts in divorce cases. We are including a description of this method to be complete.

The Excess Earnings Method is a derivative method stemming from what is often called the Excess Earnings Return on Assets Method. This method acquired its name from the IRS in ARM 34 and Revenue Ruling 68-609. Revenue Ruling 68-609 also refers to this methodology as the "formula approach" and asserts that "the formula approach may be used for determining the fair market value of intangible assets of a business only if there is no better basis therefore available."

This method combines the income and asset based approaches to arrive at a value of a closely held business. Its theoretical premise is that the total estimated value of a business is the sum of the values of the adjusted net assets (as determined by the Adjusted Book Value Method) and the value of the intangible assets. The determination of the value of the intangible assets of the business is done by capitalizing the earnings of the business that exceed a "reasonable" return on the adjusted (identified) net assets of the business.

The premise of method is that valuation can be broken into value due to Tangible Assets and value due to Intangible Assets.

The first step is to determine the overall expected earnings of the company. These earnings are the adjusted earnings before taxes called the normalized or adjusted Pre-Tax Income.   This calculation is done from an adjusted income statement that has to be reconciled.

The tangible net assets are computed from the Company's balance sheet. Only the assets that contribute to operating the company are used in this step and these assets are adjusted to reflect their value if sold in the open market.

Along with the value of the assets the method needs to know what the reasonable return on the net tangible assets is. This return is the estimate of the interest a bank might loan might be with the assets as collateral or the return we expect on earnings from assets. Typical estimates would range from 2% up to 10%.

Next the overall capitalization or discount rate for the company is determined. Many ways can be used to estimate this rate. Some methods use what is referred to as the build-up method to determine a discount rate similar to the methods using in the Income Approach. This has been covered previously in this book.

A discount rate is the expected rate of return that a "typical" investor would require based on the level of risk associated with the investment. Discount rates reflect the risk associated with achieving the expected income from an investment. The higher the perceived risk of achieving the forecast income stream, the higher the discount rate. Then the total value is computed as:
Total Value = adjusted net asset value + value due to excess earnings (or intangible assets)

Remember if you are analyzing your business due to a divorce and valuation of it is part of the court proceedings then this method will no doubt be the method the judge prefers. If you are selling under conditions of a divorce it is recommended that consult a certified business appraiser for assistance. This method is very complicated in its implementation.

Otherwise, if you are simply selling your business under other conditions then this method is not applicable.

Chapter 43 Valuation using Factor Rating

In this chapter a simplistic method of business valuation called the Factor Rating Method is discussed. It is used by some business brokers and is very intuitive in its application. The idea is estimate the capitalization rate for this type of company based on various factors. These factors serve as grades and are used to adjust the capitalization rate to reflect the unique attributes of the business.

Within the context of business valuation the capitalization rate is the expected rate of return that a "typical" investor would require based on the level of risk associated with the investment. This rate reflects the risk associated with achieving the expected income from an investment. The higher the perceived risk of achieving the forecast income stream, the higher the rate is required by the investor.

The method for estimating the value is simply

Value = Sellers Discretionary Cash Flow x Earnings Multiple

Where

Earnings Multiple = 1/ Capitalization Rate

This method to determine the earnings multiple is known as the Factor Rating Method. It is similar to the Kempner Trego method of decision making. Using this method a grade is entered for each attribute of the business and a weight of importance is specified for each of these factors.

The business is being graded based on various criteria or attributes the business has.

As an example see below how the business is graded. Each criterion is shown with its grade and its component weight. You enter the weight to give more weight to particular criteria or attribute. You will give a higher weight to most important. You grade the business from 0 to 10 of how well it meets the criteria or attribute.

Grade (High 10, Average 5 , Low 0)	Grade(0-10)	Relative Weight
Historical Profit (marginal, erratic, stable)	5.00	1.00
Income Risk (high, medium, low)	5.00	1.00
Terms of Sale (cash, normal, above market)	5.00	1.00
Business Type (service, service &retail, distributor)	5.00	1.00
Business Growth (flat, slight, high)	5.00	1.00
Location and Facilities (poor,average,good)	5.00	1.00
Diversification (limited,average,high)	5.00	1.00
Marketability (few,average,many buyers)	5.00	1.00
Competition (high,average,few)	5.00	1.00
Industry Growth (flat,slight,high)	5.00	1.00

The grade can be 0 through 10 with 10 the best grade. The relative weight is simply how important this criterion is to you, the valuator.

If a selected criterion is more important than another it should be given a higher weight.

An earnings multiple is computed as a percentage. The highest earnings multiple possible for this business called Max Multiple. For many businesses this max multiple is three.

Using the grades and the weights the evaluated earnings multiple is computed as:

Earnings Multiple $= \Sigma_i$ (Grade$_i$ x Weight x Max Multiple/10)/ (Σ_i Weight$_i$)

Where i $= 1$ to 10

The maximum multiple is typically three (3.0) for most businesses and the maximum grade is 10. The number of grades or factors is 10.

One can see that the Factor Rating Method allows one to estimate the company desirably by breaking the company down into numerous factors. Each factor is given a weighting. The weights may be adjusted based on your criterion.

Once each factor is graded then the capitalization rate is computed.

Once the earnings multiple is estimated, then a value is estimated using the following formula.

Value $=$ Seller Discretionary Cash flow * Earnings Multiple

Chapter 44 How to use Financial Ratios

In the Market Approach you will need to rate or compare your business against other companies of the same type. You will have to decide if your company is average, below average or above average. You can rate your company to determine what quartile it may fall into with respect to the performance of other companies. The comparison data will consist of sales multiples (sales price to earnings) and these multiples will range from high to low where the better companies are the higher multiples.

The calculation and study of your company's financial ratios will help you rate your company and determine where in the range of multiples your company belongs.

You can also compare your financials ratios to the financial ratio data published by Robert Morris and Associates (RMA data) to see how your company compares to the overall industry for your type of business. RMA data is readily available to the public.

Below each of the important financial ratio calculations and an explanation of each as to their importance are given.

Current Ratio = Total Current Assets / Total Current Liabilities

Generally this metric measures the overall liquidity position of a company. It is certainly not a perfect barometer, but it is a good one. Watch for big decreases in this number over time. Make sure the accounts listed in 'current assets' are collectible. The higher the ratio, the more liquid the company is.

Quick Ratio = (Currents Assets - Inventory) / Total Current Liabilities

This is another good indicator of liquidity, although by itself, it is not a perfect one. If there are receivable accounts included in the numerator, they should be collectible. Look at the length of time the company has to pay the amount listed in the denominator (current liabilities). The higher the ratio, the stronger the company using the Quick Ratio as a measure.

Debt Service Coverage= Total Liabilities / Owners Equity

This Balance Sheet leverage ratio indicates the composition of a company's total capitalization -- the balance between money or assets owed versus the money or assets owned. Generally, creditors prefer a lower ratio to decrease financial risk while investors prefer a higher ratio to realize the return benefits of financial leverage.

Interest Coverage Ratio = EBITDA / Interest Expense

This ratio measures a company's ability to service debt payments from operating cash flow (EBITDA). An increasing ratio is a good indicator of improving credit quality. The higher the better.

Debt Leverage Ratio = Total Liabilities / EBITDA

This ratio measures a company's ability to repay debt obligations from annualized operating cash flow (EBITDA).

Inventory Days = (Inventory / COGS) * 365

This metric shows how much inventory (in days) is on hand. It indicates how quickly a company can respond to market and/or product changes. Not all companies have inventory for this metric.
The lower the better.

Average Collection Days = (Accounts Receivable / Sales) * 365

This number reflects the average length of time between credit sales and payment receipts. It is crucial to maintaining positive liquidity. The lower the better.

Accounts Payable Days = (Accounts Payable / COGS) * 365

This ratio shows the average number of days that lapse between the purchase of material and labor, and payment for them. It is a rough measure of how timely a company is in meeting payment obligations. Lower is normally better.

Fixed Asset Turnover = Sales / Gross Fixed Assets

This asset management ratio shows the multiple of annualized sales that each dollar of gross fixed assets is producing. This indicator measures how well fixed assets are 'throwing off' sales and is very important to businesses that require significant investments in such assets. Readers should not emphasize this metric when looking at companies that do not possess or require significant gross fixed assets. The higher the more effective the company's investments in Net Property, Plant, and Equipment are.

Gross Profit Margin = Gross Profit / Sales

This number indicates the percentage of sales revenue that is paid out in direct costs (costs of sales). It is an important statistic that can be used in business planning because it indicates how many cents of gross profit can be generated by future sales. Higher is normally better (the company is more efficient).

Return on Assets = Net Income / Total Assets

This calculation measures the company's ability to use its assets to create profits. Basically, ROA indicates how many cents of profit each dollar of asset is producing per year. It is quite important since managers can only be evaluated by looking at how they use the assets available to them. The higher the better.

Return on Equity = Net Income / Owners Equity

This measure shows how much profit is being returned on the shareholders' equity each year. It is a vital statistic from the perspective of equity holders in a company. The higher the better.

Profit Margin = Adjusted Net Profit before Taxes / Sale

This is an important metric. In fact, over time, it is one of the more important barometers that we look at. It measures how many cents of profit the company is generating for every dollar it sells. Track it carefully against industry competitors. This is a very important number in preparing forecasts. The higher the better.

Working Capital to Sales = (Current Assets - Current Liabilities) / Sales

This evaluates the amount of working capital the company should have. It should be low for companies that sell low cost products (10% to 15%) and higher if the products cost more (20% to 25%).

Z-Score = 6.56X1 + 3.26X2 + 6.72X3 + 1.05X4

X1 = (Current Assets - Current Liabilities) / Total Assets

X2 = Retained Earnings / Total Assets

X3 = EBIT / Total Assets

X4 = Total Equity / Total Liabilities

The Z-Score is a ratio which measures the overall health of a business. In some cases, it can be used as an early predictor of a firm's probability of bankruptcy in the next year. How to interpret the Z-Score: a score of 2.60 or above implies a low risk of bankruptcy; a score between 1.10 and 2.60 is an average risk; a score of 1.10 or lower signals a high risk of bankruptcy

Chapter 45 Questions to ask when buying

How much time does the owner spend in the business per week?

What functions does the owner perform in the business?

Can the business operate without the owner?

How much of the sales are due to personal goodwill of the owner?

Who does the books?

What bookkeeping system is used in the business?

During due diligence how will the buyer see the details of the accounting system to verify the tax returns? Can the buyer see the detailed accounting system data?

The tax returns and financials indicate a cash basis of accounting. Is that correct? Or is it on accrual basis?

What were the accounts receivable and payable at the end of the last year?

What are the current accounts receivable and payable?

How much working capital is required?

Can you supply an accounts receivable aging?

How many employees and what are their job functions?

Are there any supervisors? How many? What do they supervise?

Who designs the marketing brochures? Is it an outside service?

What software do you use?

Who does the sales? How many salesmen?

How do you perform sales and marketing?

Can you breakdown your sales into classes – mailing? Services? Design? Etc...

Is there shift work involved? How many? How many people? How many shifts and people per shift?

Do any of the employees have special training?

Who does the maintenance of machinery and equipment?

What do they maintain?

Do you use any outside maintenance services on equipment? Who and how much and what do they do?

How many competitors? Who is your largest competitor?

What markets do you service geographically?

What areas of the market are your services provided and what is the percentage in each?

If the owner decides to stay on what will he require for salary?

How long will the owner train the new buyer as part of the acquisition?

It looks like the building is 10,000 sq. feet, how much is warehouse production and how much is office?

The assessed value of the building is $700,000. What is the sale price of the building and how did you arrive at that price? Is there an existing mortgage on the building?

If the buyer would lease the building what lease price and terms are you willing to provide over what period.

Why are you selling the business?

What expertise does the current owner have with respect to this business?

Who performs the daily accounting? Who does the payroll?

Can you supply an equipment list with the age and value of the equipment?

Who does the sales and how is it done? What is the sales pitch?

What was the largest order your company has received? When? How much?

How many orders do you process each year?

Can you break down the size of the orders for last year? How much of this was repeat business?

The sales appeared to have dropped slightly since two years ago and not grown, why? What can be done to increase sales?

Are there any personal owner benefits that the owner takes in the company – vacation travel, medical insurance, auto, and other expenses?

Some of the expenses have reduced or increased dramatically since past years. Why?

What metro areas in the State do you serve? How do you market these metro areas?

Who maintains the equipment? Do you have employees who can do the maintenance?

Do you have service contracts for maintaining the equipment? Are they long term contracts?

Do your employees have special training on the equipment they operate? Can they fix maintenance and operational problems?

Who designs your brochures? If you do what software do you use? Are you using mac or windows 7 or windows 8?

Are your computer systems on a network? Who maintains that?

Do you subcontract out any of your work? Who do you use and why?

Your company has quite a bit of contract work – who do you contract to? Are they long term and trained?

How do you train your sales staff? What do they have to know to begin selling your services?

Do you bid particular jobs or do you have standard rates for different services?

It appears you have considerable data processing supplies? What computer systems do you have? What do you do with regard to data processing?

Do you have any special software that has been developed by your staff or some outside company that you use in your business? What is it and how is it used?

Is any of your equipment out of date and needs to be replaced?
When is the last time you replaced a major piece of equipment?
How much inventory is included and what is it?
What is the average amount of inventory?
How often do you order supplies?

Chapter 46 Letter of Intent Sample

(Date goes here)

XYZ, Inc.
2014 Alabama Road
Miami, Florida
Attention: Mr. Bruce Jonson, President

Dear Mr. Jonson:

This letter of intent ("Letter of Intent") will confirm the proposed acquisition by the _____ ("Buyer") of the assets and real property of ZYZ, Inc., a Florida corporation (the "Company") and from Bruce Jonson (the "Owner"). The Owner, in his capacity as the seller, shall sometimes be referred to herein as the "Seller".

Based upon information you have furnished to us, the Buyer would be interested in pursuing the proposed transaction on the terms and conditions described herein.

Agreement. As promptly as possible after the execution of this Letter of Intent, the parties shall work towards the preparation and execution of a purchase agreement ("Agreement") covering the terms, types of representations, warranties, covenants, conditions, holdbacks and escrows, together with ancillary documents, necessary to accomplish the transaction, all of which must be, as to form and substance, mutually satisfactory and acceptable to the parties hereto.

Form of Transaction. The Buyer shall purchase all the assets and real property located at 2014 Alabama Road, Miami, Florida from the Owners free and clear of all liens and encumbrances.

Purchase Price. The purchase price ("Purchase Price") for the assets shall be _____ (_____), and the purchase price for the real property located at 2014 Alabama Road, Miami, Florida shall be _____(_____).

Escrow Deposit. The Buyer hereunder will pay a deposit of ten percent (10%) of the Purchase Price of the Business to Seller (the "Deposit") upon acceptance of this Letter of Intent by the Seller. This deposit will be held in Escrow and if this letter of intent is cancelled for any reason, any and all Deposit amounts shall be immediately refunded to Buyer. If the parties hereto consummate the transaction contemplated herein, any Deposit amounts shall be applied to the Purchase Price. Any Deposit shall be held by the escrow agent mutually agreed upon by Buyer and Seller.

No Assumed Liabilities. The Buyer shall assume no liabilities of any kind of the Seller.

Noncompetition Agreement. The Seller shall enter into a Noncompetition Agreement, whereby the Seller shall agree not to compete with the business of the Company for a period of five (5) years following the closing, throughout the State of Florida, or otherwise solicit customers or employees of the Company.

Duty to Maintain Purchased Assets. From the date of this Agreement through the closing, the Seller shall not deplete or waste any of the assets of the Company; it being understood that the Owners shall operate the business through closing in the normal course of business consistent with historical practices (Buyer acknowledging that the historical practice of the Company has been to distribute to the Owners the excess cash of the business).

Confidentiality. The parties shall keep the existence and terms of this Letter of Intent strictly confidential and not disclose it to any other person for any purpose, except that (i) the Buyer may disclose the existence and terms to its advisors and lenders for the sole purpose of performing its due diligence in connection with its purchase and (ii) Seller may disclose the existence and terms to its professional advisors who have a need-to-know. To the extent that a party believes disclosure is legally required, that party shall immediately notify the other parties to this Agreement and provide them with an opportunity to file an action to prevent disclosure. The Seller confirms that it has been advised by its legal counsel that, as of the date hereof, it is not required to publicly disclose this Letter of Intent or the discussions referred to herein.

Due Diligence. From and after the execution of this Letter of Intent, the Seller shall afford to the Buyer and its accountants, counsel and other representatives full off-site access to the Company and its books and records and shall furnish to the Buyer all information concerning the business, assets and properties of the Company to enable the Buyer to make such accounting, legal and audit investigations and examinations deemed desirable by the Buyer; provided (i) all due diligence shall be conducted at reasonable times and upon reasonable notice to Seller and so as to not unreasonably interfere with the business operations of the Company and (ii) any contact with employees, customers or contractors of the Company will only be done in the presence of Seller or as otherwise specifically pre-approved in writing by Seller.

Expenses. Each party shall bear its own costs and expenses (including all legal, accounting, investment banking and other costs) with respect to this transaction, regardless of whether the transaction is consummated. No expenses incurred by the Seller shall be charged against or paid out of the Company.

Exclusivity. Unless negotiations between the Buyer and the Seller are terminated (it being understood that the Seller will not unilaterally terminate negotiations as long as the Buyer is proceeding expeditiously in good faith), the Seller shall not act upon or entertain in any way any offer from any other person or entity to purchase either the Shares or any material assets of the Company or to enter into a merger or other transaction with the Seller (an "Alternate Transaction"). The Seller shall promptly (within seventy-two (72) hours) notify the Buyer upon the receipt of an unsolicited competing offer in respect of an Alternate Transaction and of the proposed terms of such offer.

Non-Binding; Termination. This Letter of Intent is a non-binding letter of intent, and serves solely to indicate the intent of the parties to come to a more formal agreement regarding the subject matter of this Letter of Intent. This Letter of Intent may be terminated by either party upon written notice if the parties fail to enter into the Agreement by November 23, 2013.

Governing Law. This Letter of Intent, the Agreement and all collateral documents shall be governed by and construed in accordance with the internal laws of the State of Florida without regard to principles of conflicts of law. Venue shall be in Monroe County, Florida.

Counterparts and Facsimile Signature. This letter of Intent may be executed in counterparts, each of which shall be deemed an original, but all of which together shall constitute one and the same instrument. A signature of a party transmitted by facsimile shall constitute an original for all purposes.

If the terms and conditions set forth above are acceptable to you, please so indicate by signing one copy of this Letter of Intent below and returning an executed original to the undersigned no later than 5:00 p.m. on October 12,

2013. If a signed original of this Letter of Intent is not returned by such date and time, this Letter of Intent shall be null and void.

Yours sincerely,

/s/   /s/

_____   _____

(Name of Buyer here)   (Name of Buyer here)

THE UNDERSIGNED ACCEPT AND AGREE WITH THE FOREGOING LETTER OF INTENT.

XYZ, Inc., a Florida corporation

By: _____

Bruce Jonson, President _____

Bruce Jonson, individually _____

Chapter 47 Contract Terms

Date of Contract	
Name of Buyer	
Name of Seller	
Business Name	
Business Address	
Purchase Price	
Earnest Money	amount of earnest money put forth with agreement
Escrow Agent	Who the agent is and address of agent
Deposit upon Acceptance	amount of deposit once this contract is signed
Cashier's Check at Closing	amount of cashier's check at closing
Seller Note Terms	Amount , interest rate , length and other conditions
Acceptance	states how long the offer is open and now the buyer can accept offer
Closing Date	defines the closing date of the sale
Closing Agent	Who the closing agent is
Closing Costs	what the closing costs are and who is paying
Closing Proration's	This is for taxes and other portions of costs between buyer and seller
Promissory Note	Security Agreement
Bill of Sale	denies the bill of sale and what it covers
Account Receivable	This describes how the accounts receivable will be handled
Inventory	describes how inventory is handled
Warranty	Defines the Seller's warranty
Indemnification	Sellers indemnifies the buyer from damages, claims, debts, etc…
Right of Set-off	Buyer will retain money for time period to secure indemnification
Accounts Payable	This describes how the accounts payable will be handled
Covenant not to Compete	defines the scope of the noncompete agreement by Seller
Financial Information	Seller warrants financial information given to buyer is correct
Buyer' Acknowledgment	Buyer is relying solely on Buyer's own inspection of Business and Seller's representations of the business

Seller's Acknowledgment	Seller has relied solely on Buyer's representations
Litigation	Except as noted herein, Seller represents and warrants that there is no judgments, liens, actions, arbitrations, decrees, investigations or proceedings
Default	If Buyer fails to perform this Contract within the time specified herein, including the payment of all deposits, the deposits paid by Buyer may be retained by Seller as liquidated damages and full settlement of any claims or the Seller may proceed in equity to enforce the Contract.
Condition of Equipment	All furniture, fixtures and equipment, and other personal property included in this sale, as set forth on Schedule "A", are being purchased on an "AS IS" basis, without warranties of its merchantability or fitness for any particular purpose. However, at the time of Closing, all equipment shall be in working condition. It is the Buyers sole responsibility to inspect the equipment prior to Closing to determine that the equipment is in working condition.
Loss or Damage	In the event there is any loss or damage to the Business premises or any of the assets, improvements, systems or equipment included in this sale at any time prior to Closing, the risk of loss shall be upon Seller.
Operation before Closing	Seller hereby agrees, from the date of execution of this contract to the date of Closing, to carry on the business activities and operations of the Business diligently and in substantially the same manner as has been customary in the past, and Seller shall not remove any items, with the exception of product inventory sold in the normal course of business.
Business Telephone	States how the telephone number will be handled
Business Mail	States how the business mail will be handled
Business Records	States how the records will be handled
Business Premises	Until Closing, Seller agrees to maintain the

	Business premises, including heating, cooling, plumbing and electrical systems and built-in fixtures, together with all other equipment and assets included in this sale, in good working order and to deliver the premises in a clean and orderly condition.
Business Deposits	Any and all amounts currently on deposit for the benefit of the Business for utility services, leases, insurance, etc., are and shall remain the sole property of Seller and are not included as part of the Purchase Price. Buyer shall, as of the date of Closing, deposit such monetary amounts as is necessary to continue the operation of the Business or the Seller shall receive a credit for such deposits at Closing.
Licenses and Permits	: Unless otherwise specified herein, Seller agrees to cooperate with Buyer in obtaining, at Buyer's expense, any licenses, permits, approvals or certificates necessary for the continued operation of the Business.
Training	This describes how much and what training the Seller will provide
Business Trade Name	Seller hereby grants Buyer, effective with the Closing of this sale, any and all rights held by Seller in the trade name
Lease of Premises	This describes the lease the Buyer will have from the Seller if there is a lease
Incorporation by Buyer	It is acknowledged and agreed that Buyer may elect to incorporate. In such event, the Buyer shall assign this Contract to the newly formed corporation. Buyer shall cause the corporation to ratify and adopt the terms and conditions of this Contract.
Pre-closing Covenants	Buyer and Seller agree not to disclose to any third party the terms and conditions of this transaction prior to the date of Closing, except to the party's attorneys, accountants or other professional advisors. Buyer further agrees not to visit the business premises prior to Closing, discuss the pending sale, contact employees, vendors or customers, without Seller's approval.
Authority	The undersigned have the full authority to

	enter into this Contract and to conclude the transaction described herein. This Agreement has been duly authorized, executed and delivered by Seller and Buyer and constitutes a legal, valid and binding obligation, enforceable against each of them in accordance with its terms.
Governing Law	Describe the state and state law this agreement is under
Escrow Disputes	Describes what happens in this instance according to State law
Waiver	No waiver of any provisions of this contract shall be effective unless it is in writing, signed by the party against whom it is asserted and any such waiver shall only be applicable to the specific instance to which it relates and shall not be deemed to be a continuing waiver.
Binding Effect	This contract shall bind and inure to the benefit of the successors, assigns, personal representatives, heirs and legatees of the parties hereto. The parties acknowledge that this Contract, including all covenants, representations, warranties and agreements, shall survive the Closing of this transaction.
Entire Agreement	Time is of the essence. This Purchase Contract constitutes the entire agreement and under-standing of the parties and cannot be modified except in writing executed by all parties. All the terms, conditions, covenants and representations made herein shall survive the Closing of this transaction.
Severability	In the event that any of the terms, conditions or covenants of this Contract are held to be unenforceable or invalid by any court of competent jurisdiction, the validity and enforceability of the remaining provisions, or portions thereof, shall not be affected thereby and effect shall be given to the remaining provisions.
Contract Review	From the date of acceptance of this Contract, Buyer and Seller shall have five (5) business days from the date of the last party to execute the Contract to have this

	Contract including all addenda or amendments, reviewed by their respective attorneys for the sole purpose of verifying that the form and language used herein adequately protects their clients and to make any necessary language changes within such time. The substance and material terms of this Contract shall remain unchanged.
Real Property	describes the real property to be sold with the business and terms of sale
Environmental	The parties acknowledge having been advised that they are aware of the health, liability and economic impact of environmental matters relative to real estate transactions, which may include the sale of the Business or the lease of the premises where the Business is conducted.
Tax Disclosure	There might be State law governing the sales tax liability of parties involved in the sale or exchange of business assets.
Contingencies	This could be bank financing or obtaining a lease, etc..
Due Diligence	Defines due diligence time period and rules and procedures
Closing Agent Instructions	Instruction on the closing agent
Date Buyer Received	
Buyer Acceptance	Signature and acceptance
Date Seller Accepted	
Seller Acceptance	Signature and acceptance

Chapter 48 Income Approach Example

The following is a detailed example for valuation of an electrical contracting company using the income approach.

A step by step example of the approach is given on the following pages.

- The adjusted financials are provided.
- The calculation of the net cash flow to equity is then demonstrated using historical data
- An example of how the discount rate and capitalization rate is given
- The theory and equations of the discounted future earnings model is summarized from the earlier discussion in the book
- Next the forecast of the future earnings is shown. It forecasts of the net cash flow earnings for the future five years earnings of the company.
- Finally, the future earnings are discounted to the present value to determine the value at the present time

First, the yearly cash flows are shown on the following page.

	2006	2005	2004	2003	2002
Sales	15,920,867	15,100,000	14,791,377	12,372,881	9,609,935
Cost of Sales	12,385,479	11,799,498	11,558,333	10,191,634	7,497,276
Gross Profit	3,535,388	3,300,502	3,233,044	2,181,247	2,112,660
Expenses					
Dep. Expense	66,593	71,948	194,280	107,990	86,843
Salaries	906,269	849,543	841,975	551,968	680,151
Repairs	36,554	50,693	56,113	43,363	36,648
Miscellaneous	5,300	4,500	3,384	6,305	12,237
Rent	121,276	117,744	114,314	110,985	85,373
Advertising	60,955	59,607	88,349	49,131	50,368
Employee Benefits	9,079	16,661	26,094	29,895	13,502
Office	70,470	80,006	47,196	15,094	59,162
Postage Shipping	12,510	13,179	12,412	14,242	13,432
Professional Fees	98,000	104,582	84,382	97,632	98,703
Supplies	15,019	15,000	15,032	26,852	14,000
Utilities	17,881	20,694	19,952	12,622	19,075
Telephone	79,204	76,167	72,588	70,041	66,841
Meals & Entertmt	79,182	65,801	54,133	48,001	48,273
Travel	91,822	81,388	116,589	25,959	24,393
Licensing	2,200	2,278	168	405	1,437
Training Education	32,558	32,048	34,998	16,062	21,374
Insurance	91,051	103,354	130,471	95,876	51,890
Contributions	360	6,782	12,623	19,856	9,874
Subscriptions	21,234	13,399	26,878	18,328	24,508
Computers	33,253	29,415	36,827	19,350	19,746
Health Insurance	32,793	34,449	0	0	0
Auto and Truck	227,311	194,454	168,295	138,421	105,351
Outside Services	22,734	30,227	71,886	79,222	20,698
Uniforms	20,100	17,846	28,911	20,172	8,908
Total Expenses	2,153,708	2,091,765	2,257,850	1,617,772	1,572,787
Net Income	1,381,680	1,208,737	975,194	563,475	539,873
Minus Interest	-64,372	-117,708	-61,365	-56,923	-49,718
Pretax Net Income	1,317,308	1,091,029	913,829	506,552	490,155
+ Excess Officer Comp	150,000	150,000	150,000	100,000	100,000
Add Other Comp.	263,000	263,000	256,000	185,000	191,000
Pretax Net Income	1,730,308	1,504,029	1,319,829	791,552	781,155

The Calculation of the Net Cash Flow to Equity is demonstrated below

	2006	2005	2004	2003	2002
Pretax Net Income	1,317,308	1,091,029	913,829	506,552	490,155
Add: Excess Officer Compensation	150,000	150,000	150,000	100,000	100,000
Add: Other Comp.	263,000	263,000	256,000	185,000	191,000
Adjusted Pretax Net Income	1,730,308	1,504,029	1,319,829	791,552	781,155
Less: Allowance for Income Taxes - 40%	692,123	-601,612	-527,932	-316,621	-312,462
Add: Depreciation & Amortization	66,593	71,948	194,280	107,990	86,843
Less: Capital Expend.	0	0	-37,483	551,968	0
+/- Changes in Long-term Debt	122,356	44,299	17,770	0	0
+/- Changes in Working Capital	-83,720	-142,053	-382,269	-357,739	0
Net Cash Flow to Equity	1,143,414	876,611	584,196	777,150	555,536

The development and computation of the discount rate is below.

Risk-Free Rate = 4.60 %

Equity Risk Premium = 7.1 %

Size Premium = 4.4 %

Company Specific Risk Premium = 2.5 %

Total Discount Rate = 4.6%+7.1%+4.4%+2.5% = 18.6%

Total Discount Rate = 19% rounded

Sustainable Long-Term Growth = 4.0%

Capitalization Rate = 19% - 4.0% = 15%

The Total Company Specific Risk Premium is computed as follows:

Industry Risk = 0%
Financial Position = 0%
Level of Diversification = 1.0%
Depth of Management = .5%
Competition = 1.0%
Barrier to Funds = 0%
Expected Growth = 0%

Total Company Specific Risk Premium = 2.5%

The development of the company specific risk is determined by the judgement of the person performing the valuation. In this case the determination was done as follows.

Industry Risk - the overall industry is not risky compared to other industries, the company is within a niche market where their expertise is needed and it is hard for competitor's to enter so a 0% has been assigned

Financial Risk – the company's financial position is not very risky, it has very little debt and overhead, financial ratios look good when compared to Industry – a 0% risk is assessed

Level of Diversification – the company is not diversified – 1% was assessed

Depth of Management – the company does have some depth in management but there is risk here – assessment is .5%

Competition – there are no immediate competitors in the area but competitors can enter – a 1.0% assessment results

Barrier to Funds – there are startup costs and bonding required, there is a barrier to funding for other companies – the assessment was 0%

Expected Growth – growth is expected , company serves needed support systems for Florida's growth and is needed – a 0% assessment

Discounted Future Earnings Equation

The selection of one of the two income methods to use depends on the stability of the projected cash flow. For purposes of demonstration of the Discounted Future Earnings method is used. The demo assumes a future cash flow has been selected that will vary each year. In the case where the cash flow and growth is stable the Single Period Capitalization Method would be used.

$$PV = \Sigma_i\ (R_i\ /\ (1+k)^i\ +\ (R_n*(1+g))/((k-p)*(1+k)^n)$$

This method converts future series of benefits into value brought to the present value at a rate of return that reflects the risk inherent in the benefit stream. This rate is called the discount rate. The model applies if the earnings are unstable and there is not a constant sustainable growth. It applies when the Single Period Capitalization Method does not.

The model consists of two stages. The first is applied to a forecast of a number of year's n. The expected cash flows R_i and discounted to a present value. The second stage consists of an estimate of the terminal value of the business at year n. Then this value is discounted from year n to the present with a discount factor shown above.

PV = present value k = discount rate

R_i = return for that year it is the net cash flow to equity (NFCE)

i represents a particular year in the model

g is the long term sustainable growth

n = number of years into the future for forecast typically five years

The last part of the summation is the terminal value of the investment at year n brought forward to the present.

The idea is to model the amount of cash that can be removed from the business without impairing its future operations. As we discussed before this is called Net Free Cash Flow or Net Cash Flow to Equity (NFCE)to be more exact. This goes along with the idea in the Income Approach that treats valuation as an investment analysis.

The NFCE is the return on the equity and is computed as follows.

Adjusted Pretax Income = Net Income before Taxes + Normalization Adjustments

Normalized Income after Taxes = Adjusted Pretax Income – Allowance for Taxes

Gross Cash Flow = Normalized Income after Taxes – Depreciation + Amortization

Net Cash Flow to Equity = Gross Cash Flow + Changes in Working Capital + Changes in Long Term Debt - Capital Expenditures to support future

A summary of these calculations are shown on the spreadsheet on the following page with the equation for discounting the future cash flows implemented in a spreadsheet for the final estimated value using the income approach.

The following is a calculation of the net free cash flow to equity.

	2007	2008	2009	2010	2011
Adjusted Pretax Net Income	1,736,856	1,597,470	1,595,617	1,732,679	1,904,623
-: Allow for Taxes - 40%	-694,742	-638,988	-638,247	-693,071	-761,849
+: Dep. & Amort.	66,924	60,232	66,255	72,880	80,168
-: Cap. Expend.		100,000	100,000	100,000	100,000
+/- Changes in Long-term Debt					
+/- Changes in Working Capital		100,000	100,000	100,000	100,000
Net Cash Flow to Equity	1,109,037	1,218,714	1,223,625	1,312,487	1,422,942
Net Cash Flow to Equity	1,143,414	876,611	584,196	777,150	555,536

The calculation of value based on the cash flows for year is shown below.

Year	Forecasted Cash Flow		19.0% Rate Value Factors		Present Value Future Cash Flow
1st Year	1,109,037	x	0.91670	=	1,016,653
2nd Year	1,218,714	x	0.77033	=	938,818
3rd Year	1,223,625	x	0.64734	=	792,102
4th Year	1,312,487	x	0.54398	=	713,971
5th Year	1,422,942	x	0.45713	=	650,468
Terminal Value	7,788,735	x	0.45713	=	3,560,456
Total Value					7,672,467

Chapter 49 Market Approach Example

The idea behind the market approach is that the value of a business can be determined by reference to reasonably comparable guideline companies ("comps") for which transaction values are known. The values may be known because these companies are publicly traded or because they were recently sold and the terms of the transaction were disclosed.

For a business valuation professional, a good set of comparables would normally be a minimum of three. One of the objectives in analyzing comparables is to determine if the comparable company has a similar profile.

The Direct Market Data Method of the Market Approach focuses on transactions involving the sales of entire companies. Since the transactions comprise sales of entire companies.

Private company data is frequently available but with limited amounts of detail. In fact, the most often used multiples (ratios) available from these private databases are the selling price to the annual gross revenue and the selling price to some form of earnings or income stream.

Some of the databases provide only limited information about the business—business SIC code, a short description about its line of business, annual revenue, selling price, and some form of earnings.

One of the advantages to the market approach is the apparent simplicity in implementing it. The basic format is:

Value = (Price/Parameter)$_{comp}$ x (Parameter of subject)

(For invested capital multiples, debt should be subtracted.) The first part of the pricing multiple is the numerator — the price measure of the comparable company. The denominator can be any number of income streams, i.e. Price/Revenue, Price/EBITDA, Price/ Seller's Discretionary Cash Flow, other cash flows or financial statistics.

A number of organizations collect and disseminate information on transactions. Most publications make their databases accessible on the Internet for a fee on a per-use basis or annual subscription access. Among the most widely used are shown below:

Name	No. of Records	Median Revenue	Median Price	Public or Private	Source
IBA Data	30,000			Private	Brokers
BIZCOMPS	9,000	360,000	135,000	Private	Brokers
Pratt's Stats	8,606	1,600,000	1,500,000	Private & Public	Brokers
Done Deals	7,300		1M - 1Billion	79% Private	SEC financial
Mid-Market Comps	7,300		1M- 1 Billion	79% Private	SEC financial
Done Deals and Mid-Market Comps 50% of transactions under $15M (25 data points per transaction) , IBA stands for Institute of Business Appraisers					
Pratt Stats deal price range from $500K to $14.5Billion , 3,800 private companies and 250 public companies (up to 81 data points per transaction)					
IBA and BIZCOMPS cover relatively small companies (less than $100K to $2 Million					

The Institute of Business Appraisers (IBA) databases are studies of small business sales whereby relevant pricing information is collected from business brokers and transaction intermediaries on individual sales of small businesses. The IBA database is the largest known source of market transactions of small closely held businesses. It contains about 30,000 transactions with 680 SIC codes. The data base is geared to small businesses. The transactions are all asset sales and the selling price does not include the cash, accounts receivable and accounts payable. It does include inventory. The reported sales price but does include an estimate of value for furniture, fixtures and equipment and compensation and owners benefits for one owner.

Bizcomps was first produced by Jack R. Sanders, a business broker in San Diego. The information is gathered from business brokers by Standard Industrial Classification ("SIC") category. The transactions are all asset sales and the selling price does not include the cash, accounts receivable, accounts payable and inventory. The reported sales price does not include inventory, but does include an estimate of value for furniture, fixtures and equipment. The estimated value for inventory and furniture, fixtures and equipment are reported separately. The owner compensation and benefits are included in the price.

Pratt's Stats® covers both main street businesses and larger M&A transactions. 46% of the 8,606 deals in the Pratt's Stats® database are businesses that sold for $1,000,000 or less. 54% of the 8,606 deals in the Pratt's Stats® database are businesses that sold for between $1,000,001 and $500,000,000. The median selling price in Pratt's Stats® is $1,500,000. Pratt's Stats® data includes up to 81 data fields. Pratt's Stats® sales can be either an asset sale or stock sale. For an asset sale, the Pratt's Stats® selling price generally includes inventory and generally excludes cash, accounts receivable and accounts payable. The appraiser may determine what assets transferred in the Pratt's Stats® sale by looking at the Asset Data. For a stock sale, the Pratt's Stats® selling price generally includes all operating assets and liabilities.

An example criterion used to search for comparative market data for closely held sales transaction data is shown below.

Industry:	SIC code 1731- Special trade contractors primarily engaged in electrical work at the site.
Types of Transaction:	Controlling interests. (Little or no market for non-controlling interests in closely held companies)
Time:	Transactions closed between January 1, 1985 and the effective date of the valuation.
Standard of Value:	Fair market value transactions in which the buyers were financial buyers and not strategic buyers.
Domicile:	U. S. Corporations

The results of the search are provided below for each database.

Data Base	No Trans.	Sale Price to Earnings			
		Low	High	Mean	Median
IBA	52	0.72	5.68	1.95	1.71
BIZCOMPS	30	0.98	5.68	2.32	2.12
Pratt Stats	26	1.12	9.74	5.90	6.06

The Table below shows the indicated value using the method. Even though each data base contained a sufficient number of transactions, it was decided to use the Pratt Stat's Median value of the Price to Earnings multiple for the following reasons: BIZCOMPS and IBA contain many transactions for small companies not comparable to the subject company. Pratt Stat's had sufficient transactions, were closer to the subject company's size, provided detailed information on each company and these were all stock transactions.

The selected multiple was the median equity price-to-earnings multiple of 6.06 based on stock transactions. The Fair Market Value is computed below.

Forecasted Pre-Tax EBT (using forecast for 2006 = 1,692,286
Median Derived Multiple (from Pratt Stats) = 6.06
Fair Market Value on a Control, Non-Marketable Basis = 10,259,000

Chapter 50 Market Statistics - Cash Flow Multiples

The statistics associated with various types of businesses are presented below. We have listed the SIC and NAICS classification codes and the average Seller's Discretionary Cash Flow (SDCF) and the Cash Flow multiples for various types of businesses along with the average size business as measured in sales.

It shows the average multiple with the statistics hi and low with the average sales volume the statistics were based on. The average sales volume serves as a check for companies of similar size. This table is based on small companies. For medium to large size companies an order of magnitude larger we can expect the multiple will be higher.

The multiple is defined as Multiple = Business Value / SDCF

Assume we have a carpet cleaning company that is doing $200,000 in sales.

Then from the table we see the Multiple = 1.7

The expected value is then   Value = 1.7 x 200,000 = 340,000

It has a range of 2.49 x 200,000 = 498,000   on the high side.

If you believe the carpet cleaning is a great company and has many years' experience in business then a good estimate of value may be half way between the average of $340,000 and the high of $498,000 which would be $419,000 for the expected value.

Business Description	SIC	NAICS	Average Multiple	Hi	Low	Average Sales
Adult Home Care	7363	56132	2.73	5.54	0.00	1,582,188
Advertising Sales	7319	54183	2.01	3.88	0.15	364,000
Aircraft Services	4581	561720	3.21	5.91	0.51	895,667
AircraftRepair&Main	3724	336412	2.20	3.70	0.71	1,135,000
Ambulance Service	4119	62191	3.20	7.62	0.00	580,651
Amusement Ride	7999	71399	5.62	19.44	0.00	592,800
Architectural Design	8712	54131	1.65	2.53	0.77	763,143
Asphalt Service	1611	23411	3.78	9.66	0.00	2,166,000
Assisted Living	8051	62311	1.77	3.23	0.31	676,550
Assisted Living	8059	62311	1.29	1.29	1.29	532,000
Audio Visual Production	7812	51211	3.74	8.90	0.00	418,636
Auto Dealership	5511	44111	6.02	16.51	0.00	4,333,334
Auto Detail Service	7542	811192	2.40	4.56	0.25	586,014
Auto Glass Repair	7536	811122	1.70	2.38	1.03	231,750
Auto Glass Replacement	5231	44419	2.38	5.12	0.00	926,659
Auto Muffler Shop	7533	811112	2.01	3.41	0.60	1,010,714
Auto Paint Shop	7532	811121	1.91	3.39	0.44	668,281
Auto Rental	7514	532111	2.06	3.59	0.54	1,144,500
Auto Repair Shop	7538	811111	2.18	5.01	0.00	541,489
Auto Trans Repair	7537	811113	1.74	2.94	0.54	549,432
Beauty Salon	7231	812112	12.60	55.18	0.00	341,757
Billiard Parlor	7935	71399	1.92	3.13	0.71	236,000
Bindery	2789	323121	2.36	2.99	1.73	217,333
Boat & Motor Dealer	5551	441222	2.69	7.10	0.00	1,772,306
Boat Marina	4493	71393	6.94	13.13	0.75	929,750
Book Store-Christian	5942	451211	1.40	2.33	0.47	389,300
Bowling Alley	7933	71395	2.44	5.55	0.00	378,000
Bulldozing Service	5039	44419	2.14	3.03	1.26	6,324,600
Car Rental/Sales	7515	53211	2.10	3.03	1.17	482,000
Carpet Clean Equip Rental	7359	532412	0.97	6.58	0.00	490,862
Carpet Cleaning	7217	56174	1.70	2.49	0.91	286,783
Catering Business	5812.299805	72232	2.27	5.69	0.00	631,107
CateringTruckRoute	5812.310059	72232	1.22	1.52	0.92	156,667
Charter Tour Airline	4522	48799	2.57	2.57	2.57	3,089,000
Check Cashing Service	6099	523999	2.41	4.39	0.43	391,667
Chiropractic Practice	8041	62131	1.41	2.20	0.62	571,875
Chrome Plating	3471	332813	2.49	5.88	0.00	822,333
Civil Engineering	8710	54133	2.87	2.87	2.87	677,000
CivilEngrWater	8711	54133	2.14	3.78	0.51	1,875,375
Clinical Monitoring	8071	621511	1.54	2.69	0.39	872,000
Closet Organizer	2519	337143	2.75	5.71	0.00	1,063,833
Cocktails W/Food	5813	72241	2.16	4.73	0.00	412,487
Coffee House	5812.259766	722211	2.32	4.51	0.12	287,170
Coin Laundry	7215	81231	2.69	4.88	0.51	137,910
Cold Storage	4222	49312	2.33	3.23	1.42	1,551,000
Comedy Club	7922	71111	1.37	1.83	0.92	500,750
Comm Paper Route	5963	45439	2.03	2.70	1.37	155,800
Computer Rental	7377	53242	0.79	1.68	0.00	1,004,500

166

Business Description	SIC	NAICS	Average Multiple	Hi	Low	Average Sales
Computer Software	7372	51121	3.02	3.88	2.15	1,000,000
Computer Training	8243	611519	2.99	4.68	1.30	1,104,500
Concrete Contractor	1771	23571	2.44	3.90	0.97	2,754,167
Concrete Sawing	1795	23594	3.32	4.78	1.87	948,250
Const Equi Service	7353	532411	1.71	3.12	0.29	472,000
Construct Manage	8741	23332	1.91	3.21	0.60	2,640,000
ContrComm Flooring	1752	23552	1.54	2.24	0.83	1,752,231
ContrCustomCabinet	1751	23551	1.92	3.25	0.59	1,039,111
ContrDrilling Service	1781	23581	1.29	2.69	0.00	587,750
Contr-Drywall	1742	23542	2.01	2.82	1.20	2,388,500
ContrElectrical	1731	23531	2.02	3.89	0.15	1,737,930
Contr-ElectricMaint	1732	223531	3.50	3.50	3.50	1,200,000
Contr-Excavation	1794	23593	3.11	6.45	0.00	2,340,000
ContrFireFldRestore	1799	23599	2.20	3.72	0.67	992,815
ContrHeating & AC	1711	23511	2.41	5.38	0.00	1,046,543
ContrHomeImprove	1521	23592	1.92	3.58	0.27	1,312,269
Contr-Masonary	1741	23541	1.70	3.72	0.00	1,088,250
Contr-Painting	1721	23521	1.50	2.44	0.55	766,269
Contr-Roofing	1761	23561	2.06	3.40	0.73	2,008,324
ContrSteel Builgs	1541	23332	2.09	3.59	0.59	3,957,900
ContrTenantImprov	1522	23332	1.61	1.61	1.61	2,681,000
Contr-Tile/Marble	1743	23543	1.84	2.98	0.71	1,020,750
Contr-Tree Service	783	56173	2.31	4.01	0.61	339,400
Convention Consult	8748	54169	2.85	4.02	1.67	778,500
Cookie Franchise	5461	722213	2.81	6.51	0.00	382,472
Copy Shop	7334	561431	2.23	3.42	1.04	328,364
Courier Service	7399	492110	2.39	3.44	1.35	687,333
CPA Practice	8721	541211	2.12	3.92	0.32	192,083
CreditReportAgency	7323	56145	1.85	1.85	1.85	552,000
Dance Studio	7911	611610	3.63	8.12	0.00	181,000
DataProcesServices	7374	51421	2.84	6.75	0.00	1,484,500
Day Care Center	8351	62441	2.12	4.01	0.22	345,289
Day Spa & Salon	7991	71394	2.38	6.82	0.00	350,990
Deli Restaurant	5812.209961	722211	1.82	4.13	0.00	338,481
Deli-Bagels	5812.25	722211	2.07	4.26	0.00	477,345
DeliIndust WCater	5812.22998	722211	1.76	2.42	1.10	231,600
DeliOffice Building	5812.240234	722211	1.59	2.41	0.76	190,556
Deli-Sandwiches(3)	5812.220215	722211	2.20	4.32	0.07	282,761
Dental Laboratory	8072	339116	1.69	2.50	0.88	487,800
Dental Practice	8021	62121	1.00	1.06	0.93	410,000
DesignBuild/Pricing	1542	23332	2.17	2.17	2.17	663,000
Detective Services	7381	561611	3.52	8.48	0.00	832,042
DiaperCleanSupply	7219	81149	0.00	0.00	0.00	85,000
Direct Mail/Printing	7331	54186	1.67	3.23	0.11	495,276
DistrAdvert Special.	5110	54181	1.79	2.88	0.70	698,000
Distr-Apparel Acc.	5131	42231	2.92	2.92	2.92	1,213,000
Distr-Appliances	5064	42162	1.49	2.80	0.18	1,757,143
DistrBeerBeverage	5181	42281	3.31	5.65	0.96	515,333
Distr-Brand Sandals	5139	442340	1.50	1.50	1.50	1,890,000
DistrCDRec. Equip	5084	42183	2.33	4.62	0.04	1,938,733
Distr-Ceramic Tiles	5032	42132	1.00	1.00	1.00	6,900,000

Business Description	SIC	NAICS	Average Multiple	Hi	Low	Average Sales
DistrConst Products	5085	42184	2.21	3.77	0.64	1,962,649
Distr-Doors & Windows	5031	44419	1.72	2.74	0.70	1,825,250
Distr-Dry Food Products	5141	42241	1.97	3.23	0.71	1,653,342
Distr-Durable Goods	5072	42171	3.04	5.04	1.05	882,778
Distr-Electronic Equipment	5065	42169	1.71	2.78	0.63	2,411,938
Distr-Electronics	5043	42161	1.41	2.54	0.28	9,388,667
Distr-Frozen Food	5142	42242	1.70	3.29	0.10	689,500
Distr-Gifts/Glassware	5199	42299	1.82	3.41	0.23	1,097,600
Distr-Golf Turf Equip	5083	44421	1.29	2.59	0.00	4,639,600
Distr-Heating Oil	5171	454311	6.01	13.71	0.00	2,038,750
Distr-Heating Oil	5983	454311	5.94	7.72	4.17	1,902,667
Distr-Home Furnishings	5023	42122	1.87	2.92	0.82	1,921,000
Distr-Industrial Tires	5014	44132	3.25	3.25	3.25	2,400,000
Distr-Janitorial Supplies	5087	42185	2.13	3.74	0.53	743,795
Distr-Laser Products	5112	42212	1.95	4.05	0.00	741,333
Distr-Lighting Products	5063	42161	2.08	3.65	0.50	2,868,714
Distr-Medical Supplies	5047	42145	2.36	3.92	0.80	1,655,629
Distr-Motion Pic	7822	51212	2.29	2.29	2.29	333,000
DistrOffice Equip	5044	42142	2.60	4.78	0.42	1,122,333
DistrPackaging Prod	5113	42213	2.00	3.49	0.51	1,351,917
Distr-Potato Chips	5145	42245	1.09	1.09	1.09	300,000
Distr-Propane	5172	42272	5.08	10.66	0.00	3,687,818
Distr-Propane	5984	454312	7.11	7.11	7.11	4,201,000
Distr-Sheet Metal	5075	42173	1.67	1.67	1.67	1,363,000
Distr-Snack Foods	5149	42249	2.10	4.30	0.00	473,333
DistrTobacco Prod	5194	422940	1.70	2.82	0.58	1,910,667
Distr-Video Games	5092	42192	1.46	2.76	0.17	1,097,583
Distr-Whsle Jewelry	5094	42194	1.24	2.24	0.24	775,571
Distr-Writing Paper	5111	531221	1.83	2.22	1.43	1,489,000
Document Preparation	8399	813212	2.10	3.06	1.13	273,500
Donut Shop	5462	311811	2.90	7.17	0.00	939,650
Dry Clean W/Laundry	7216	812322	2.56	4.67	0.44	348,549
Educational Tutoring	8211	61111	2.88	5.33	0.42	315,833
Electronic Repair	7622	811212	1.65	3.09	0.21	562,625
Elevator Service	1796	23595	1.59	1.59	1.59	945,000
Embroidery Service	2395	314999	2.46	4.03	0.89	629,750
Employment Agency	7361	56131	2.72	5.23	0.21	1,696,200
Engraving Service	7341	461499	1.43	1.67	1.19	218,000
EnvirTestingAsbestos	8734	54138	2.40	2.82	1.99	1,452,000

Business Description	SIC	NAICS	Average Multiple	Hi	Low	Average Sales
Environmental Cleanup	8731	54133	2.90	5.13	0.68	2,852,667
Exporter	9999	99999	1.51	1.51	1.51	703,000
Factoring Company	6159	522298	2.31	2.31	2.31	1,358,000
Fast Food-Chicken	5812.1401377	722211	1.70	2.59	0.80	255,000
Fast Food-Franchise	5812.1098637	722211	2.22	4.54	0.00	393,650
Fast Food-Hamburgers	5812.1201177	722211	2.88	5.74	0.01	607,595
Fast Food-Ice Cream	5812.1601567	722211	3.82	10.25	0.00	258,724
Fast Food-Juice Bar	5812.1899417	722211	1.85	3.51	0.19	314,714
Fast Food-Mexican	5812.1499027	722211	2.09	4.70	0.00	419,423
Fast Food-Pizza	5812.1298837	722211	2.18	5.33	0.00	372,485
Fast Food-Sno-Cones	5812.1801767	722211	2.61	3.90	1.33	139,250
Fast Food-Yogurt	5812.1699227	722211	1.86	2.84	0.88	195,700
FEDEX Ground Route	4215	48423	1.74	1.74	1.74	55,000
Finance Company	6141	522291	1.56	2.28	0.85	592,000
Franchisor-Baby Supplies	6794	53311	3.05	6.32	0.00	170,667
Freight Forwarding	4413	484121	1.49	1.49	1.49	340,000
Frozen Fruit Processor	2037	311411	1.87	2.32	1.41	2,704,000
Garbage Collection	4950	0	1.89	1.89	1.89	135,000
Golf Course-9 Hole	7992	71391	2.47	4.90	0.04	765,857
Graphic Design	7336	54143	2.23	4.38	0.09	634,636
Graphic Art/Printing	2754	323111	2.03	2.06	2.00	363,000
Hair Cutting Salon(2)	7241	812112	1.82	4.02	0.00	350,667
Hi-Tech Sales Consultants	8732	54191	4.98	10.35	0.00	3,090,000
Home Center	5251	44413	1.78	4.09	0.00	751,323
Home Health Care	8082	62161	3.60	6.14	1.05	1,171,600
Home Water Delivery	4941	22131	4.23	8.85	0.00	116,000
Industrial Linen Rental	7213	812331	1.74	2.12	1.37	328,500
Industrial Packaging	4783	488991	2.22	2.99	1.44	777,000
Install-Windows & Doors	1793	23592	1.85	3.12	0.58	1,461,231
Inst-Fire Alarm Systems	7382	561621	2.94	3.99	1.88	2,885,000
Institutional Pharmacy	5122	42221	10.03	10.03	10.03	11,343,000
Insurance Agency	6411	55421	1.83	3.48	0.17	418,364
Internet Diaper Sales	5137	42331	1.85	2.32	1.39	499,000
Internet Marketing Co	7379	514191	1.75	3.26	0.24	512,118
Internet Related	7375	541512	3.40	3.64	3.16	6,065,500
Internet Service Provider	7179	514191	2.76	3.17	2.35	1,040,500
Internet-Computer Batteries	5045	42144	1.67	3.49	0.00	1,769,000
Janitorial Service	7349	56172	1.72	2.91	0.53	425,746
Jewelry Repair	7631	81149	1.79	2.43	1.15	345,000

169

Business Description	SIC	NAICS	Average Multiple	Hi	Low	Average Sales
Judicial Supervision	9229	92219	1.33	1.33	1.33	127,000
L/D Trucking	4213	484122	2.58	4.77	0.40	1,124,019
Land Surveying	8713	54136	1.60	2.31	0.88	533,200
Landscape-Commercial	781	56173	2.18	3.31	1.06	4,722,000
Landscape-Design/Const	782	56173	1.86	3.36	0.35	654,550
Landscaping Service	7350	56172	0.44	0.44	0.44	60,000
Laundry Service	7211	812321	3.01	6.94	0.00	423,000
Legal Practice	8111	54111	2.01	2.78	1.25	421,000
Live-in Child Care	8322	62419	1.70	1.70	1.70	104,000
Lube & Tune-up	7549	811191	2.29	4.86	0.00	509,417
Lumber Treatment	2491	321114	0.00	0.00	0.00	2,000,000
Magazine Franchise	2721	51112	1.83	2.74	0.91	199,800
Magazine Publisher	2741	51199	2.16	4.52	0.00	433,030
Mail Order Business	5961	45411	2.02	4.29	0.00	1,381,333
Man. Training/Consulting	8742	541612	1.43	2.50	0.37	623,800
Marine Towing Service	4492	48833	3.23	5.91	0.55	581,500
Marketing/Advertising	7311	54181	1.70	2.96	0.43	875,136
Massage School	8299	611699	1.63	3.35	0.00	490,846
Media Relations Firm	8743	541820	1.93	1.93	1.93	1,577,000
Medical Claims Recovery	7322	56144	2.71	3.78	1.65	1,073,714
Medical Testing	8099	821512	1.66	2.93	0.39	531,182
Medical Transportation	4338	561492	0.00	0.00	0.00	1,030,000
Metal Heat Treating	3398	332811	4.00	4.00	4.00	3,000,000
Mfg & Design - Aquariums	3231	327215	2.10	3.10	1.09	1,627,000
Mfg/Distr-Buttons	3965	339993	1.00	1.00	1.00	312,000
Mfg/Distr-Die-cut Gift Bags	2679	322231	2.94	6.86	0.00	410,000
Mfg/Distr-Drilling Fluids	2992	324191	1.69	1.69	1.69	2,632,000
Mfg/Distr-Indust Coatings	3479	332812	2.65	4.47	0.84	618,545
Mfg/Distr-Phone Cords	3661	33421	0.87	2.11	0.00	3,139,667
Mfg/Distr-Restr Supplies	5046	42144	1.41	2.73	0.10	1,079,000
Mfg/Distr-Shampoo	2844	32562	2.13	3.40	0.87	210,000
Mfg/Distr-Steel Fab	5035	44419	2.05	2.72	1.38	13,716,000
Mfg/Install-Boat Lifts	3448	332311	2.34	3.77	0.90	672,000
Mfg/Retail-Furniture	2511	337122	2.73	5.34	0.12	1,171,214
Mfg/Whsle-Hobby Supplies	3944	339932	2.11	3.68	0.54	580,667
Mfg-Agricultural Product	3274	32741	2.47	2.47	2.47	2,438,000
Mfg-Aircraft HVAC	3728	336412	1.63	3.81	0.00	2,349,333
Mfg-Aluminum Fabrication	3355	331319	3.10	6.03	0.17	865,600
Mfg-Apparel	2311	315211	2.05	4.59	0.00	1,616,091
Mfg-Archery Products	3421	332211	3.36	3.36	3.36	1,500,000
Mfg-Automotive Products	3714	336312	1.87	3.00	0.74	935,571
Mfg-Bed Linens	2399	323999	2.35	2.35	2.35	2,323,000
Mfg-Blower Systems	3564	333411	2.45	5.14	0.00	1,332,000
Mfg-Bottled Soft Drinks	2086	312111	2.33	2.33	2.33	816,000
Mfg-Bulk Pasta	2098	311823	3.32	4.55	2.09	1,061,000
Mfg-Cabinets	2434	337131	1.72	3.01	0.43	768,952
Mfg-Ceramic Products	3269	327112	2.27	3.57	0.97	608,400
Mfg-Chemicals	2819	325998	2.73	4.51	0.95	1,902,429
Mfg-Chocolate	2066	31132	2.36	2.57	2.14	282,000
Mfg-Chocolate	2064	31132	2.75	2.75	2.75	139,000
Mfg-Cleaning Products	2841	325611	1.77	1.77	1.77	144,000
Mfg-Composted Humus	2875	325314	2.45	2.55	2.36	672,000

170

Business Description	SIC	NAICS	Average Multiple	Hi	Low	Average Sales
Mfg-Computer Peripherals	3575	334113	0.76	0.76	0.76	511,000
Mfg-Concrete Recycling	2951	324121	6.17	6.17	6.17	1,200,000
Mfg-Concrete Vibrators	3531	33312	1.94	4.54	0.00	1,037,667
Mfg-Connectors	3674	334413	4.62	5.51	3.73	8,100,000
Mfg-Cultered Marble	3281	327991	2.28	4.30	0.26	1,195,095
Mfg-Custom Drapes	2391	314121	2.55	5.51	0.00	217,333
Mfg-Custom Rubber Products	3061	326291	0.73	2.18	0.00	1,354,500
Mfg-Electr Test Equip	3825	334515	2.42	2.42	2.42	784,000
Mfg-Electronic Products	3571	334311	1.06	1.06	1.06	170,000
Mfg-Electronics	3672	334412	2.28	4.05	0.52	1,065,273
Mfg-Electronics	3625	335314	4.90	11.56	0.00	1,795,143
Mfg-Elevator Product	3534	333921	3.13	3.13	3.13	596,000
Mfg-Fastening Tools	3545	333515	3.08	4.30	1.86	2,525,000
Mfg-Fiberglass Handles	3423	332212	2.76	3.34	2.18	1,154,500
Mfg-Fiberglass Products	3999	326199	0.93	7.18	0.00	1,009,143
Mfg-Fiberglass Truck Parts	3713	336211	2.23	3.77	0.69	1,768,667
Mfg-Food Processing	2035	311411	4.17	4.17	4.17	18,000,000
Mfg-Gears	3566	333612	0.00	0.00	0.00	500,000
Mfg-Handicap Vehicles	3711	336211	2.07	2.07	2.07	1,260,000
Mfg-Hats Mittens etc	2353	315991	0.00	0.00	0.00	154,000
Mfg-Health Food	2099	311999	3.41	4.80	2.02	490,000
Mfg-Hog Feeders, Etc.	3523	333111	0.76	0.76	0.76	150,000
Mfg-Hot Pads/Oven Mitts	2390	314999	2.22	2.22	2.22	1,411,000
Mfg-Ice Products	2097	312113	2.29	3.06	1.53	317,500
Mfg-Indust Process Equipment	3823	33453	3.81	3.81	3.81	650,000
Mfg-Instrument Accessory	3931	339992	3.79	3.79	3.79	1,752,000
Mfg-Interior Fixtures	3354	331316	2.69	4.42	0.96	1,384,667
Mfg-Iron Works	3446	332323	1.86	2.28	1.44	708,429
Mfg-Jewelry	3911	339911	0.67	1.33	0.02	490,000
Mfg-Leather Tanning	3111	31611	1.62	1.62	1.62	200,000
Mfg-Lighting Product	3645	335121	1.45	1.45	1.45	400,000
Mfg-Log Home Prefabs	2452	321992	2.64	3.72	1.57	2,193,000
Mfg-Machine Shop	3599	33271	2.66	5.17	0.15	1,097,237
Mfg-Mail Box Locks	3429	332439	1.06	1.06	1.06	259,000
Mfg-Marine Products	3732	336612	1.64	3.37	0.00	1,522,000
Mfg-Marking Devices	3953	339943	2.59	2.59	2.59	311,000
Mfg-Measuring Devices	3629	335999	0.56	0.56	0.56	1,030,000
Mfg-Medical Products	3357	331422	1.97	4.46	0.00	916,000
Mfg-Men?s Clothing	2329	315225	2.31	4.69	0.00	928,000
Mfg-Metal Products	3441	332312	2.83	5.90	0.00	1,771,750
Mfg-Metal Stamping	3444	332322	2.72	6.20	0.00	2,455,678
Mfg-Mexican Sauces	2032	311422	2.93	2.93	2.93	2,200,000
Mfg-Mineral Wool Insulation	3296	327993	3.47	3.47	3.47	30,000,000
Mfg-OEM Products	3399	332999	2.46	2.46	2.46	634,000
Mfg-Office Furniture	2521	337134	2.42	3.82	1.02	1,629,000
Mfg-Oilfield Equipment	3533	333132	0.00	0.00	0.00	2,000,000
Mfg-Ophthalmic Goods	3851	339115	3.58	3.58	3.58	1,731,000
Mfg-Ornamental Iron	3449	332323	2.80	3.90	1.70	1,035,600

Business Description	SIC	NAICS	Average Multiple	Hi	Low	Average Sales
Mfg-Outdoor Accessories	3299	327999	1.16	2.95	0.00	472,667
Mfg-Outdoor Products	3949	33992	2.53	5.17	0.00	2,746,000
Mfg-Paint Products	2851	32551	2.53	4.70	0.36	336,333
Mfg-Paper Products	2671	322221	2.79	3.32	2.26	1,833,667
Mfg-Paper Products	2621	322121	1.77	3.00	0.55	2,815,000
Mfg-Pet Bedding	2299	31321	0.00	0.00	0.00	1,735,000
Mfg-Picture Frames	3952	337139	2.82	3.59	2.04	1,013,000
Mfg-Plastic Injection	3089	326199	1.95	3.11	0.79	661,000
Mfg-Plastic Products	3079	326121	2.64	4.67	0.62	2,154,350
Mfg-Popcorn Products	2096	311919	2.41	3.54	1.28	255,500
Mfg-Power Cylinders	3593	33271	6.31	6.31	6.31	9,423,000
Mfg-Power Plant Products	3699	335313	3.22	4.76	1.67	3,472,800
Mfg-Pumps	3561	333912	1.38	1.38	1.38	1,162,000
Mfg-Refrigeration Equipment	3585	333415	2.57	5.38	0.00	2,335,875
Mfg-Roll Shutters	2899	321999	4.19	8.82	0.00	671,500
Mfg-Rubber Aprons	2384	315211	1.68	1.68	1.68	125,000
Mfg-Rubber Pet Products	3069	326299	1.50	1.50	1.50	220,000
Mfg-Screw Machining	3451	332721	2.92	3.36	2.48	1,791,000
Mfg-Security Systems	3671	334411	3.67	3.67	3.67	1,500,000
Mfg-Sheet metal	3443	332322	1.83	4.26	0.00	1,915,667
Mfg-Signal Processing Equip	3679	334419	3.75	3.75	3.75	2,600,000
Mfg-Snack Foods	2068	311911	1.39	1.39	1.39	750,000
Mfg-Software	7371	541511	2.49	5.34	0.00	1,026,929
Mfg-Solar/Security Film	3081	326113	3.81	3.81	3.81	24,000,000
Mfg-Spa Covers	2394	314912	1.84	3.67	0.01	523,118
Mfg-Specialty Food	2047	311111	2.67	5.91	0.00	493,667
Mfg-Specialty Product	3499	332999	2.54	4.77	0.31	868,824
Mfg-Stereo Speakers	3651	33431	1.37	1.37	1.37	158,000
Mfg-Store Fixtures	2541	337131	0.75	2.25	0.00	2,977,000
Mfg-Styrofoam Products	3086	32615	2.86	4.32	1.41	1,734,286
Mfg-Terrariums	3962	339999	1.84	1.84	1.84	190,000
Mfg-Textile Equipment	3552	33319	1.81	1.81	1.81	4,000,000
Mfg-Textile Printing Equip	3559	333319	2.99	6.01	0.00	4,912,500
Mfg-Tool & Die	3544	333514	2.59	4.29	0.89	2,668,231
Mfg-Tool & Die	3541	333514	1.43	2.71	0.15	641,750
Mfg-Trailers	3721	336212	3.31	5.23	1.38	7,100,000
Mfg-Trophy Awards	5999	453999	1.79	3.80	0.00	512,317
Mfg-Truck Products	3465	33637	1.21	1.21	1.21	610,000
Mfg-Trusses	2439	321214	2.76	3.37	2.14	1,249,333
Mfg-Turquoise Refining	3915	339913	1.53	1.53	1.53	339,000
Mfg-Vibrating Screens	3569	333999	4.15	4.15	4.15	2,900,000
Mfg-Vinyl Notebooks	2678	322233	2.56	2.56	2.56	355,000
Mfg-Weight Loss Suppl	2833	325411	1.89	1.89	1.89	1,410,000
Mfg-Wheel Chairs	3842	339113	1.93	5.09	0.00	504,500
Mfg-Wind Measure Device	3829	334519	3.17	5.66	0.68	1,937,500
Mfg-Window Coverings	5714	442291	1.88	2.92	0.84	627,667
Mfg-Window Coverings	2591	33792	2.44	4.16	0.72	798,750
Mfg-Windows	2431	321911	2.38	5.12	0.00	1,476,500
Mfg-Windshield Cleaner	2842	325612	1.48	2.54	0.42	949,000

Business Description	SIC	NAICS	Average Multiple	Hi	Low	Average Sales
Mfg-Wood Pallets	2448	32192	2.69	4.06	1.31	1,314,000
Mfg-Wood Products	2499	321999	2.36	3.90	0.82	1,599,837
Mfr-Motors/Generators	3621	335312	2.54	2.54	2.54	742,000
Mini-Mart W/Gas/Wash	5541	44711	2.25	4.87	0.00	1,982,132
Mobil Disk Jockey	7929	71119	1.04	1.04	1.04	67,000
Mobile Advertising	7312	54182	1.15	2.13	0.18	401,000
Motorcycle Dealership	5571	441221	2.39	5.01	0.00	3,076,367
Movie Theater-2 Screens	7832	512131	0.55	3.26	0.00	324,667
MRI Examinations	8093	621498	1.87	2.38	1.37	1,046,333
Mud Jacking Service	1389	213113	1.18	1.18	1.18	239,000
Office Equipment Repair	7378	811212	1.20	2.33	0.06	100,500
One Hour Photo	7384	812922	1.98	3.36	0.61	523,333
Parking Lot Sweeping	4959	562998	1.81	2.52	1.10	369,273
Parking Services	7521	812930	1.61	1.61	1.61	383,000
Party Photographers	7221	541921	1.75	2.49	1.01	337,667
Pest Control	7342	56171	1.81	3.35	0.28	213,929
Pet Grooming/Boarding	752	81291	1.95	3.67	0.23	194,767
Photo Studio-Little Leagues	7335	541922	1.46	1.71	1.21	294,500
Plastic Lamination	3083	32613	1.90	1.90	1.90	226,000
Plant Grower	181	111421	1.69	2.97	0.40	980,333
Pool Cleaning Service	7389	56179	1.97	3.42	0.52	335,793
Pre-Stress Concrete	3272	32739	2.53	4.36	0.70	922,143
Print/Glue/Fold Cardboard	2675	322298	2.08	3.77	0.39	640,375
Printing - Forms	2761	323116	5.78	5.78	5.78	800,000
Printing Accounting Forms	2759	323119	0.97	1.27	0.66	132,500
Printing Shop	2752	323114	2.35	3.96	0.74	638,103
Public Scales	4785	448490	1.74	1.74	1.74	54,000
Radiator Repair Shop	7539	811118	1.64	2.65	0.63	415,438
Radio Broadcast Station	4832	513112	32.57	81.71	0.00	325,500
RE Sales/Property Man.	6531	53121	2.06	3.33	0.79	532,314
Recreational Park	7033	721211	2.09	3.00	1.17	383,000
Recycling-Anti-Freeze	5093	42193	1.94	3.44	0.45	832,529
Redimix U-Hau Concrete	3273	32732	3.16	5.42	0.90	825,750
Refrigeration Repair	7623	811211	3.49	6.22	0.76	406,500
Remfg-Indust Comp.	3563	333912	1.71	4.00	0.00	288,500
Rental-Cellular Phones	4813	51333	0.84	5.54	0.00	1,286,267
Restr W/Cocktails	5812.009766	72211	2.89	7.50	0.00	766,723
Restr-Asian	5812.069824	722211	1.40	4.65	0.00	851,143
Restr-Breakfast/Lunch	5812.040039	722211	1.59	2.89	0.28	252,421
Restr-Coffee Shop	5812.049805	722211	2.22	3.88	0.57	306,000
Restr-Dinner house	5812.02002	72211	3.20	7.28	0.00	590,944
Restr-Family	5812.029785	722211	2.07	4.15	0.00	598,152
Restr-Greek Food	5812.080078	722211	1.98	3.39	0.58	246,500
Restr-Italian	5812.089844	722211	1.91	3.76	0.06	473,202
Restr-Mexican	5812.100098	722211	1.97	3.80	0.13	401,806
Restr-Seafood	5812.060059	722211	2.24	4.39	0.10	1,037,318
Restr-Vegetarian	5812	722211	4.88	11.41	0.00	233,000
Retail Property Lessors	6512	53112	1.07	1.07	1.07	620,000
Retail/Mail Order-CD?s	5735	45122	1.60	1.60	1.60	258,000
Retail-Appliances	5722	44311	1.47	2.28	0.66	516,143

Business Description	SIC	NAICS	Average Multiple	Hi	Low	Average Sales
Retail-Arts & crafts	5945	45112	1.73	3.23	0.22	462,742
Retail-Candy & Nuts	5441	445292	1.62	2.53	0.70	219,417
Retail-Cellular Phones	4812	513321	1.84	3.34	0.34	787,971
Retail-Children'Furniture	5021	44211	1.50	1.59	1.41	652,000
Retail-Clothing	5621	44812	1.68	4.09	0.00	429,347
Retail-Electronics	5731	44312	1.69	2.48	0.89	741,143
Retail-Fabrics	5949	45113	2.93	6.14	0.00	576,500
Retail-Feed Store	5991	44422	2.48	2.56	2.40	1,964,000
Retail-Floor Coverings	5713	44221	1.90	3.36	0.43	1,079,676
Retail-Florist	5992	45311	1.97	4.27	0.00	301,870
Retail-Furniture	5712	337133	1.81	3.39	0.23	1,097,535
Retail-Garden Store	5261	44422	1.94	3.62	0.27	1,340,556
Retail-Gifts	5947	45322	2.03	4.18	0.00	358,464
Retail-Golf Carts	5088	42186	1.64	2.70	0.59	837,846
Retail-Grocery/Deli	5411	44511	2.02	4.63	0.00	749,733
Retail-Health Products	5499	446191	1.73	2.72	0.74	337,476
Retail-Jewelry	5944	44831	2.25	5.04	0.00	367,600
Retail-Kitchenware	5719	442299	1.84	3.36	0.32	777,474
Retail-LawnGard. Equip	5086	44421	1.16	1.16	1.16	680,000
Retail-Liquor Store	5921	44531	2.68	5.22	0.14	865,786
Retail-Lumber/Hardware	5211	42131	1.92	3.73	0.11	1,968,500
Retail-Men?s Clothes	5611	44811	1.77	3.33	0.20	774,500
Retail-Music Store	5736	45114	1.20	2.10	0.30	346,286
Retail-Newstand	5994	451212	1.79	2.85	0.73	576,500
Retail-Office Supply	5943	45321	3.44	9.39	0.00	614,167
Retail-Optical Store	5995	44613	1.68	3.20	0.17	503,000
Retail-Outdoor Equipment	5941	45111	1.90	3.96	0.00	600,106
Retail-Pharmacy	5912	44611	1.66	3.24	0.08	1,269,333
Retail-Photo & Cameras	5946	44313	0.91	0.98	0.83	591,500
Retail-Shoes	5661	44821	1.16	1.98	0.35	731,222
Retail-Spas/Billiards	5091	42191	2.48	4.16	0.80	2,064,800
Retail-Sports Apparel	5699	44819	1.42	2.56	0.28	468,304
Retail-Tires & Rims	5531	44132	1.61	4.03	0.00	776,606
Retail-Tobacco Shop	5993	453991	2.40	5.81	0.00	740,300
Retail-Used Clothing	5632	44819	2.00	3.33	0.67	221,667
Retail-Used Office Furn	5932	45331	1.89	2.73	1.04	670,000
Retail-Variety Store	5331	45299	1.65	3.12	0.19	1,397,944
Retail-Wedding Clothes	5821	44812	1.38	1.38	1.38	202,000
Ret-Child Clothes(2Loc)	5641	44813	1.88	4.02	0.00	686,143
Reupholstery Shop	7641	81142	1.71	2.83	0.58	468,632
RV Dealership	5561	44121	2.20	4.32	0.09	3,647,889
Sale/Serv-Air Compr	5082	42181	20.00	72.79	0.00	1,513,375
Sales/Serv-Computers	5734	44312	2.41	5.36	0.00	1,486,071
Sales/Serv-Electric Motors	4063	44419	1.58	1.58	1.58	755,000
Sales-Agri/Const Trailers	5599	941229	1.60	3.77	0.00	5,143,500
Secretarial Service	7338	561492	2.41	5.73	0.00	297,472

174

Business Description	SIC	NAICS	Average Multiple	Hi	Low	Average Sales
Ship Repair/Dry Dock	3731	336611	4.81	4.81	4.81	4,325,000
Shoe Repair	7251	81143	1.94	2.26	1.62	49,500
Sign Manufacturer	3993	33995	2.49	4.77	0.21	564,000
Sign Rental & Installation	7390	56179	2.17	2.17	2.17	154,000
Silk Screen Printing	2396	323113	2.04	3.22	0.86	515,756
Ski Lodge	7011	721211	1.91	1.91	1.91	240,000
Soil Decontamination	1629	23493	1.35	1.81	0.88	1,026,667
Spec Medical Practice	8011	621111	1.47	2.86	0.09	744,167
Sports Therapy Center	8049	62134	1.66	3.60	0.00	500,667
Steel Erection	1791	23591	2.04	3.40	0.69	1,849,714
Steel Processing	3325	331513	8.25	8.25	8.25	1,826,000
Storage Lockers	4225	53115	1.84	4.38	0.00	280,333
Swim Club W/Lessons	7941	711211	1.40	1.40	1.40	91,000
Tanning Salon	7299	812199	1.99	3.67	0.31	242,045
Tax and Bookkeeping	8921	541219	1.78	2.98	0.58	222,556
Taxi Cab Fleet	4121	48531	1.49	2.75	0.23	672,000
Telecom Cabling	1623	23492	3.28	7.22	0.00	4,635,462
Telephone Repair	7629	811211	1.51	2.57	0.45	530,750
Title Insurance	6361	524127	2.21	3.42	1.01	621,154
Title Insurance	6541	524127	1.61	1.61	1.61	271,000
Tract Home Builder	1531	23321	0.41	0.41	0.41	10,733,000
Transportation Consultants	4731	541614	1.43	1.43	1.43	200,000
Trash Containers	4953	562219	3.14	6.34	0.00	539,857
Travel Agency	4724	56151	2.21	4.33	0.09	1,432,118
Travel Tour Operator	4725	56152	2.28	3.50	1.05	3,175,750
Trucking Company	4212	484122	0.50	6.98	0.00	991,500
Typesetting Service	2791	323122	1.89	1.89	1.89	192,000
Used Car Dealer	5521	44112	1.65	2.28	1.02	754,800
Used Lab Equipment	5049	446199	2.10	2.10	2.10	1,814,000
Vending Machines	5962	45421	2.32	4.01	0.63	263,545
Vending-Stuffed Animals	7993	71312	2.17	3.24	1.10	402,500
Veterinary Clinic	742	54194	2.99	4.25	1.72	339,167
Video Tape Duplication	7819	51211	3.72	3.72	3.72	307,000
Video Tape Rental	7841	53223	1.88	3.30	0.46	221,377
Vocational Trade School	8249	611519	11.51	45.62	0.00	452,611
Warehouse & Crating	4226	49311	2.05	2.05	2.05	394,000
Warranty Insur Carriers	6399	524128	0.16	0.16	0.16	147,000
Water Purification	2834	325412	7.01	21.94	0.00	1,309,500
Water Treatment	8999	71151	2.01	3.71	0.31	328,500
Welding Repair Business	7699	81131	1.61	3.14	0.09	356,541
Welding-Trailer Hitches	7692	81149	1.33	2.67	0.00	213,000
Whlse-Tropical Fish	5154	42252	1.35	1.35	1.35	275,000
Whlse-Bakery	5481	311811	1.51	2.84	0.19	246,000
Whlse-Blown Glass	3229	327212	1.29	1.29	1.29	360,000
Whlse-Bread Bakery	2051	311812	2.26	3.16	1.37	596,429
Whlse-Durable Goods	5099	42131	2.24	3.82	0.66	1,109,056
Whlse-Eyeglass Frames	5048	421460	1.07	1.07	1.07	234,000
Whlse-Farm Supplies	5191	42291	-0.90	10.53	0.00	998,909
Whlse-HVAC Products	5074	42172	2.57	3.63	1.50	2,033,000

Business Description	SIC	NAICS	Average Multiple	Hi	Low	Average Sales
Whsle-Ice Cream	5147	42249	1.23	1.61	0.84	686,400
Whsle-Liquor	5182	42281	1.58	1.58	1.58	746,000
Whsle-Nursery	5193	42293	2.14	3.89	0.40	941,083
Whsle-Produce	5148	42248	2.23	3.40	1.06	2,689,750
Whsle-Seafood	5421	45439	2.07	3.61	0.52	1,315,429
Whsle-Truck Parts	5013	44131	1.82	3.31	0.33	1,026,034
Wireless Telcom	4899	513322	1.69	2.86	0.52	508,750

Chapter 51 Market Statistics - Sales Multiples

This table shows the statistics for various types of businesses based on the sales. It shows the average multiple with the statistics hi and low with the average sales volume the statistics were based on. The average sales volume serves as a check for companies of similar size.

The multiple is defined as Multiple = Business Value / Sales

Assume we have an auto repair company that is doing $200,000 in sales.

Then from the table we see the Multiple = .39

The expected value is then   Value = .39 x 200,000 = 78,000

It has a range of .72 x 200,000 = 144,000 on the high side.

If you believe the repair shop is a great company and has many years' experience in business then a good estimate of value may be half way between the average of $78,000 and the high of $144,000 which would be $111,000 for the expected value.

Business Description	SIC	NAICS	Average Multiple	Hi	Low	Average Sales
Adult Home Care	7363	56132	0.48	0.98	0.00	1,582,188
Advertising Sales	7319	54183	0.59	0.87	0.31	364,000
Aircraft Services	4581	561720	0.53	1.06	0.01	895,667
Aircraft-Repair & Maint	3724	336412	0.28	0.42	0.14	1,135,000
Ambulance Service	4119	62191	0.69	1.20	0.18	580,651
Amusement Ride	7999	71399	0.70	1.47	0.00	592,800
Architectural Design	8712	54131	0.47	0.62	0.33	763,143
Asphalt Service	1611	23411	0.53	1.04	0.02	2,166,000
Assisted Living	8051	62311	0.52	0.97	0.07	676,550
Assisted Living	8059	62311	0.40	0.40	0.40	532,000
Audio Visual Production	7812	51211	0.97	2.00	0.00	418,636

Business Description	SIC	NAICS	Average Multiple	Hi	Low	Average Sales
Auto Dealership	5511	44111	0.09	0.22	0.00	4,333,334
Auto Detail Service	7542	811192	1.03	2.09	0.00	586,014
Auto Glass Repair	7536	811122	0.56	0.73	0.38	231,750
Auto Glass Replac.	5231	44419	0.37	0.72	0.02	926,659
Auto Muffler Shop	7533	811112	0.50	0.89	0.10	1,010,714
Auto Paint Shop	7532	811121	0.42	0.77	0.06	668,281
Auto Rental	7514	532111	0.49	0.72	0.26	1,144,500
Auto Repair Shop	7538	811111	0.39	0.72	0.06	541,489
Auto Trans Repair	7537	811113	0.36	0.62	0.11	549,432
Beauty Salon	7231	812112	3.40	15.38	0.00	341,757
Billiard Parlor	7935	71399	0.59	0.87	0.31	236,000
Bindery	2789	323121	0.76	1.14	0.38	217,333
Boat & Motor Dealer	5551	441222	0.41	1.05	0.00	1,772,306
Boat Marina	4493	71393	2.25	4.67	0.00	929,750
Book Store-Christian	5942	451211	0.29	0.58	0.01	389,300
Bowling Alley	7933	71395	1.27	2.36	0.18	378,000
Bulldozing Service	5039	44419	0.47	0.77	0.17	6,324,600
Car Rental/Sales	7515	53211	0.76	1.10	0.41	482,000
Carpet Clean Rental	7359	532412	0.81	1.40	0.22	490,862
Carpet Cleaning	7217	56174	0.53	0.91	0.16	286,783
Catering Business	5812.299805	72232	0.39	0.77	0.01	631,107
Catering Truck Route	5812.310059	72232	0.48	0.81	0.16	156,667
Charter Tour Airline	4522	48799	0.50	0.50	0.50	3,089,000
Check Cashing Service	6099	523999	0.66	1.34	0.00	391,667
Chiropractic Practice	8041	62131	0.80	1.38	0.22	571,875
Chrome Plating	3471	332813	0.48	1.07	0.00	822,333
Civil Engineering	8710	54133	0.31	0.31	0.31	677,000
Civil E.-Water Related	8711	54133	0.56	0.98	0.14	1,875,375
Clinical Monitoring	8071	621511	0.47	0.94	0.01	872,000
Closet Organizer	2519	337143	0.43	0.79	0.06	1,063,833
Cocktails W/Food	5813	72241	0.45	0.83	0.07	412,487
Coffee House	5812.259766	722211	0.43	0.77	0.10	287,170
Coin Laundry	7215	81231	0.97	1.73	0.21	137,910
Cold Storage	4222	49312	0.71	1.25	0.17	1,551,000
Comedy Club	7922	71111	0.19	0.32	0.06	500,750
Comm. Paper Route	5963	45439	1.21	1.52	0.91	155,800
Computer Rental	7377	53242	0.37	1.03	0.00	1,004,500
Computer Software	7372	51121	0.49	1.30	0.00	1,000,000
Computer Training	8243	611519	0.70	1.71	0.00	1,104,500
Concrete Contractor	1771	23571	0.43	0.73	0.13	2,754,167
Concrete Sawing	1795	23594	1.09	1.40	0.78	948,250
Const Eq. Service	7353	532411	0.32	0.47	0.16	472,000
Construct Mgt.	8741	23332	0.52	1.01	0.02	2,640,000
Contr-Comm Flooring	1752	23552	0.34	0.58	0.09	1,752,231
Contr-Custom Cabinets	1751	23551	0.43	0.78	0.08	1,039,111
Contr-Drilling Service	1781	23581	0.42	0.63	0.21	587,750
Contr-Drywall	1742	23542	0.32	0.57	0.06	2,388,500
Contr-Electrical	1731	23531	0.46	0.82	0.10	1,737,930
Contr-Electrical Maint	1732	223531	0.73	0.73	0.73	1,200,000

Business Description	SIC	NAICS	Average Multiple	Hi	Low	Average Sales
Contr-Excavation	1794	23593	0.56	0.90	0.22	2,340,000
Contr-Fire/Flood Restore	1799	23599	0.48	0.93	0.03	992,815
Contr-Heating & AC	1711	23511	0.34	0.67	0.01	1,046,543
Contr-Home Improvement	1521	23592	0.39	0.72	0.05	1,312,269
Contr-Masonary	1741	23541	0.39	0.86	0.00	1,088,250
Contr-Painting	1721	23521	0.37	0.69	0.05	766,269
Contr-Roofing	1761	23561	0.37	0.63	0.11	2,008,324
Contr-Steel Buildings	1541	23332	0.32	0.74	0.00	3,957,900
Contr-Tenant Improvements	1522	23332	0.28	0.28	0.28	2,681,000
Contr-Tile/Marble	1743	23543	0.42	0.60	0.25	1,020,750
Contr-Tree Service	783	56173	1.05	2.36	0.00	339,400
Convention Consultant	8748	54169	0.79	1.24	0.34	778,500
Cookie Franchise	5461	722213	0.39	0.67	0.10	382,472
Copy Shop	7334	561431	0.70	1.18	0.23	328,364
Courier Service	7399	492110	0.61	1.15	0.07	687,333
CPA Practice	8721	541211	0.95	1.33	0.57	192,083
Credit Reporting Acy	7323	56145	0.58	0.58	0.58	552,000
Dance Studio	7911	611610	0.69	0.85	0.53	181,000
Data Process Services	7374	51421	0.80	1.98	0.00	1,484,500
Day Care Center	8351	62441	0.50	0.96	0.04	345,289
Day Spa & Salon	7991	71394	0.69	1.31	0.08	350,990
Deli Restaurant	5812.20996	1722211	0.41	0.65	0.16	338,481
Deli-Bagels	5812.25	722211	0.35	0.57	0.13	477,345
Deli-Indust. Cater.	5812.22998	722211	0.49	0.74	0.23	231,600
Deli-Office Building	5812.24023	4722211	0.52	0.80	0.25	190,556
Deli-Sandwiches(3)	5812.22021	5722211	0.42	0.72	0.12	282,761
Dental Laboratory	8072	339116	0.55	1.04	0.07	487,800
Dental Practice	8021	62121	0.54	0.88	0.20	410,000
Design/Build/Pricing	1542	23332	0.42	0.42	0.42	663,000
Detective Services	7381	561611	0.56	1.23	0.00	832,042
Diaper Clean/Supply	7219	81149	0.75	0.75	0.75	85,000
Direct Mail/Printing	7331	54186	0.46	0.95	0.00	495,276
Distr-Advert Special.	5110	54181	0.53	1.22	0.00	698,000
Distr-Apparel Acc.	5131	42231	0.50	0.50	0.50	1,213,000
Distr-Appliances	5064	42162	0.24	0.57	0.00	1,757,143
Distr-Beer & Bev.	5181	42281	0.64	1.08	0.20	515,333
Distr-Brand Sandals	5139	442340	0.32	0.32	0.32	1,890,000
Distr-CD Record Eq.	5084	42183	0.37	0.69	0.05	1,938,733
Distr-Ceramic Tiles	5032	42132	0.22	0.22	0.22	6,900,000
Distr-Const Products	5085	42184	0.32	0.67	0.00	1,962,649
Distr-Doors& Wind.	5031	44419	0.39	0.78	0.00	1,825,250
Distr-Dry Food Prod.	5141	42241	0.38	0.79	0.00	1,653,342
Distr-Durable Goods	5072	42171	0.40	0.65	0.14	882,778
Distr-Electron Equipt	5065	42169	0.35	0.79	0.00	2,411,938
Distr-Electronics	5043	42161	0.17	0.26	0.08	9,388,667

Business Description	SIC	NAICS	Average Multiple	Hi	Low	Average Sales
Distr-Frozen Food	5142	42242	0.56	1.23	0.00	689,500
Distr-Gifts/Glassware	5199	42299	0.35	0.72	0.00	1,097,600
Distr-Golf Turf Equip	5083	44421	0.46	1.06	0.00	4,639,600
Distr-Heating Oil	5171	454311	0.35	0.69	0.01	2,038,750
Distr-Heating Oil	5983	454311	0.46	0.87	0.05	1,902,667
Distr-Home Furnish	5023	42122	0.35	0.63	0.06	1,921,000
Distr-Industrial Tires	5014	44132	0.27	0.27	0.27	2,400,000
DistrJanitorial Supply	5087	42185	0.41	0.82	0.01	743,795
Distr-Laser Products	5112	42212	0.49	1.12	0.00	741,333
DistrLightingProducts	5063	42161	0.35	0.70	0.00	2,868,714
DistrMedical Supplies	5047	42145	0.49	0.97	0.02	1,655,629
Distr-Motion Pictures	7822	51212	1.15	1.15	1.15	333,000
DistrOfficeEquipment	5044	42142	0.36	0.64	0.09	1,122,333
Distr-Packaging Prod	5113	42213	0.32	0.53	0.12	1,351,917
Distr-Potato Chips	5145	42245	0.40	0.40	0.40	300,000
Distr-Propane	5172	42272	0.70	1.72	0.00	3,687,818
Distr-Propane	5984	454312	0.75	0.75	0.75	4,201,000
Distr-Sheet Metal	5075	42173	0.16	0.16	0.16	1,363,000
Distr-Snack Foods	5149	42249	0.45	0.96	0.00	473,333
DistrTobaccoProducts	5194	422940	0.17	0.32	0.01	1,910,667
Distr-Video Games	5092	42192	0.34	0.64	0.04	1,097,583
Distr-Whsle Jewelry	5094	42194	0.29	0.73	0.00	775,571
Distr-Writing Paper	5111	531221	0.35	0.46	0.24	1,489,000
DocumentPreparation	8399	813212	0.73	1.65	0.00	273,500
Donut Shop	5462	311811	0.52	0.90	0.14	939,650
Dry Clean W/Laundry	7216	812322	0.71	1.14	0.29	348,549
Educational Tutoring	8211	61111	0.81	1.84	0.00	315,833
Electronic Repair	7622	811212	0.32	0.57	0.08	562,625
Elevator Service	1796	23595	0.14	0.14	0.14	945,000
Embroidery Service	2395	314999	0.58	1.02	0.14	629,750
Employment Agency	7361	56131	0.48	0.85	0.10	1,696,200
Engraving Service	7341	461499	0.70	1.42	0.00	218,000
Envir. Testing-Asbestos	8734	54138	0.70	1.24	0.16	1,452,000
Environmental Cleanup	8731	54133	0.58	0.86	0.30	2,852,667
Exporter	9999	99999	0.34	0.34	0.34	703,000
Factoring Company	6159	522298	1.29	1.29	1.29	1,358,000
Fast Food-Chicken	5812.1401	37722211	0.37	0.64	0.10	255,000
Fast Food-Franchise	5812.1098	63722211	0.40	0.67	0.14	393,650
Fast Food-Hamburgers	5812.1201	17722211	0.43	0.69	0.17	607,595
Fast Food-Ice Cream	5812.1601	56722211	0.55	0.97	0.14	258,724
Fast Food-Juice Bar	5812.1899	41722211	0.44	0.71	0.16	314,714
Fast Food-Mexican	5812.1499	02722211	0.41	0.66	0.16	419,423
Fast Food-Pizza	5812.1298	83722211	0.33	0.54	0.11	372,485
Fast Food-Sno-Cones	5812.1801	76722211	0.81	1.39	0.23	139,250
Fast Food-Yogurt	5812.1699	22722211	0.44	0.63	0.26	195,700
FEDEX Ground Route	4215	48423	1.46	1.46	1.46	55,000
Finance Company	6141	522291	0.64	1.08	0.21	592,000
FranchisorBaby Supplies	6794	53311	1.72	4.32	0.00	170,667

Business Description	SIC	NAICS	Average Multiple	Hi	Low	Average Sales
Freight Forwarding	4413	484121	0.34	0.34	0.34	340,000
Frozen Fruit Processor	2037	311411	0.51	0.74	0.29	2,704,000
Garbage Collection	4950	0	0.74	0.74	0.74	135,000
Golf Course-9 Hole	7992	71391	0.73	1.15	0.32	765,857
Graphic Design	7336	54143	0.52	1.03	0.01	634,636
GraphicArt/Printing	2754	323111	0.44	0.65	0.23	363,000
Hair Cutting Salon(2)	7241	812112	0.37	0.71	0.03	350,667
Hi-Tech Sales Consultants	8732	54191	1.33	3.56	0.00	3,090,000
Home Center	5251	44413	0.22	0.47	0.00	751,323
Home Health Care	8082	62161	0.40	0.59	0.20	1,171,600
Home Water Delivery	4941	22131	2.37	6.08	0.00	116,000
Industrial Linen Rental	7213	812331	0.53	0.85	0.21	328,500
Industrial Packaging	4783	488991	0.66	0.79	0.53	777,000
Install-Windows& Doors	1793	23592	0.35	0.58	0.13	1,461,231
Inst-Fire Alarm Systems	7382	561621	0.73	1.01	0.45	2,885,000
Institutional Pharmacy	5122	42221	0.40	0.40	0.40	11,343,000
Insurance Agency	6411	55421	0.73	1.50	0.00	418,364
Internet Diaper Sales	5137	42331	0.37	0.56	0.17	499,000
Internet Marketing Co	7379	514191	0.58	1.29	0.00	512,118
Internet Related	7375	541512	0.78	1.87	0.00	6,065,500
Internet Serv Provider	7179	514191	0.92	1.26	0.58	1,040,500
Internet Compute Battery	5045	42144	0.34	0.80	0.00	1,769,000
Janitorial Service	7349	56172	0.54	0.95	0.13	425,746
Jewelry Repair	7631	81149	0.53	0.72	0.34	345,000
Judicial Supervision	9229	92219	0.63	0.63	0.63	127,000
L/D Trucking	4213	484122	0.65	1.33	0.00	1,124,019
Land Surveying	8713	54136	0.51	0.78	0.25	533,200
Landscape-Commercial	781	56173	0.43	0.99	0.00	4,722,000
Landscape-Design/Const	782	56173	0.54	0.95	0.14	654,550
Landscaping Service	7350	56172	0.18	0.18	0.18	60,000
Laundry Service	7211	812321	0.66	1.44	0.00	423,000
Legal Practice	8111	54111	0.65	1.11	0.18	421,000
Live-in Child Care	8322	62419	0.61	0.61	0.61	104,000
Lube & Tune-up	7549	811191	0.49	0.93	0.06	509,417
Lumber Treatment	2491	321114	0.04	0.04	0.04	2,000,000
Magazine Franchise	2721	51112	0.75	1.36	0.14	199,800
Magazine Publisher	2741	51199	0.79	1.36	0.22	433,030
Mail Order Business	5961	45411	0.48	1.08	0.00	1,381,333
Man. Training/Consulting	8742	541612	0.52	0.98	0.06	623,800
Marine Towing Service	4492	48833	1.61	3.58	0.00	581,500
Marketing/Advertising	7311	54181	0.44	0.90	0.00	875,136
Massage School	8299	611699	0.56	1.04	0.09	490,846
Media Relations Firm	8743	541820	0.38	0.38	0.38	1,577,000
Medical Claims Recovery	7322	56144	0.78	1.53	0.02	1,073,714

Business Description	SIC	NAICS	Average Multiple	Hi	Low	Average Sales
Medical Testing	8099	821512	0.71	1.19	0.23	531,182
Medical Transportation	4338	561492	0.49	0.49	0.49	1,030,000
Metal Heat Treating	3398	332811	0.67	0.67	0.67	3,000,000
Mfg & Design - Aquariums	3231	327215	0.44	0.77	0.11	1,627,000
Mfg/Distr-Buttons	3965	339993	0.19	0.19	0.19	312,000
Mfg/Distr-Die-cut Gift Bags	2679	322231	0.98	1.86	0.11	410,000
Mfg/Distr-Drilling Fluids	2992	324191	0.66	0.66	0.66	2,632,000
Mfg/Distr-Indust Coatings	3479	332812	0.75	1.17	0.34	618,545
Mfg/Distr-Phone Cords	3661	33421	0.10	0.28	0.00	3,139,667
Mfg/Distr-Restr Supplies	5046	42144	0.50	1.01	0.00	1,079,000
Mfg/Distr-Shampoo	2844	32562	0.42	0.45	0.38	210,000
Mfg/Distr-Steel Fab	5035	44419	0.12	0.14	0.09	13,716,000
Mfg/Install-Boat Lifts	3448	332311	0.43	0.59	0.26	672,000
Mfg/Retail-Furniture	2511	337122	0.57	1.12	0.03	1,171,214
Mfg/Whsle-Hobby Supplies	3944	339932	0.34	0.53	0.14	580,667
Mfg-Agricultural Product	3274	32741	0.46	0.46	0.46	2,438,000
Mfg-Aircraft HVAC	3728	336412	0.63	1.15	0.12	2,349,333
Mfg-Aluminum Fabrication	3355	331319	0.58	1.41	0.00	865,600
Mfg-Apparel	2311	315211	0.50	0.99	0.02	1,616,091
Mfg-Archery Products	3421	332211	0.72	0.72	0.72	1,500,000
Mfg-Automotive Products	3714	336312	0.52	0.94	0.10	935,571
Mfg-Bed Linens	2399	323999	0.20	0.20	0.20	2,323,000
Mfg-Blower Systems	3564	333411	0.36	0.62	0.10	1,332,000
Mfg-Bottled Soft Drinks	2086	312111	0.86	0.86	0.86	816,000
Mfg-Bulk Pasta	2098	311823	0.78	1.16	0.41	1,061,000
Mfg-Cabinets	2434	337131	0.41	0.80	0.02	768,952
Mfg-Ceramic Products	3269	327112	0.42	0.52	0.32	608,400
Mfg-Chemicals	2819	325998	0.59	0.87	0.31	1,902,429
Mfg-Chocolate	2066	31132	0.52	1.33	0.00	282,000
Mfg-Chocolate	2064	31132	0.40	0.40	0.40	139,000
Mfg-Cleaning Products	2841	325611	0.59	0.59	0.59	144,000
Mfg-Composted Humus	2875	325314	0.64	1.52	0.00	672,000
Mfg-Computer Peripherals	3575	334113	0.22	0.22	0.22	511,000
Mfg-Concrete Recycling	2951	324121	0.93	0.93	0.93	1,200,000
Mfg-Concrete Vibrators	3531	33312	0.73	0.79	0.66	1,037,667
Mfg-Connectors	3674	334413	1.14	1.43	0.86	8,100,000
Mfg-Cultered Marble	3281	327991	0.47	0.87	0.08	1,195,095
Mfg-Custom Drapes	2391	314121	0.23	0.64	0.00	217,333
Mfg-Custom Rubber Products	3061	326291	0.53	0.72	0.34	1,354,500
Mfg-Electr Test Equip	3825	334515	0.31	0.31	0.31	784,000
Mfg-Electronic Products	3571	334311	0.41	0.41	0.41	170,000
Mfg-Electronics	3672	334412	0.39	0.70	0.08	1,065,273
Mfg-Electronics	3625	335314	0.68	1.14	0.22	1,795,143
Mfg-Elevator Product	3534	333921	1.11	1.11	1.11	596,000
Mfg-Fastening Tools	3545	333515	0.73	1.39	0.07	2,525,000
Mfg-Fiberglass Handles	3423	332212	0.64	1.04	0.24	1,154,500
Mfg-Fiberglass Products	3999	326199	0.48	0.96	0.01	1,009,143
Mfg-Fiberglass Truck Parts	3713	336211	0.31	0.43	0.18	1,768,667
Mfg-Food Processing	2035	311411	0.44	0.44	0.44	18,000,000
Mfg-Gears	3566	333612	0.90	0.90	0.90	500,000

Business Description	SIC	NAICS	Average Multiple	Hi	Low	Average Sales
Mfg-Handicap Vehicles	3711	336211	0.35	0.35	0.35	1,260,000
Mfg-Hats Mittens etc	2353	315991	0.49	0.49	0.49	154,000
Mfg-Health Food	2099	311999	0.84	1.67	0.00	490,000
Mfg-Hog Feeders, Etc.	3523	333111	0.40	0.40	0.40	150,000
Mfg-Hot Pads/Oven Mitts	2390	314999	0.24	0.24	0.24	1,411,000
Mfg-Ice Products	2097	312113	0.56	0.85	0.27	317,500
MfgIndust ProcessEquipment	3823	33453	1.20	1.20	1.20	650,000
Mfg-Instrument Accessory	3931	339992	0.95	0.95	0.95	1,752,000
Mfg-Interior Fixtures	3354	331316	0.46	0.71	0.20	1,384,667
Mfg-Iron Works	3446	332323	0.39	0.71	0.07	708,429
Mfg-Jewelry	3911	339911	0.17	0.44	0.00	490,000
Mfg-Leather Tanning	3111	31611	0.60	0.60	0.60	200,000
Mfg-Lighting Product	3645	335121	0.69	0.69	0.69	400,000
Mfg-Log Home Prefabs	2452	321992	0.23	0.47	0.00	2,193,000
Mfg-Machine Shop	3599	33271	0.74	1.36	0.12	1,097,237
Mfg-Mail Box Locks	3429	332439	0.33	0.33	0.33	259,000
Mfg-Marine Products	3732	336612	0.42	0.92	0.00	1,522,000
Mfg-Marking Devices	3953	339943	1.75	1.75	1.75	311,000
Mfg-Measuring Devices	3629	335999	0.19	0.19	0.19	1,030,000
Mfg-Medical Products	3357	331422	0.69	1.19	0.19	916,000
Mfg-Men?s Clothing	2329	315225	0.85	1.66	0.04	928,000
Mfg-Metal Products	3441	332312	0.52	0.86	0.18	1,771,750
Mfg-Metal Stamping	3444	332322	0.66	1.32	0.00	2,455,678
Mfg-Mexican Sauces	2032	311422	0.80	0.80	0.80	2,200,000
Mfg-Mineral Wool Insulation	3296	327993	0.35	0.35	0.35	30,000,000
Mfg-OEM Products	3399	332999	0.67	0.67	0.67	634,000
Mfg-Office Furniture	2521	337134	0.31	0.46	0.17	1,629,000
Mfg-Oilfield Equipment	3533	333132	0.15	0.15	0.15	2,000,000
Mfg-Ophthalmic Goods	3851	339115	0.65	0.65	0.65	1,731,000
Mfg-Ornamental Iron	3449	332323	0.55	0.83	0.26	1,035,600
Mfg-Outdoor Accessories	3299	327999	0.23	0.33	0.14	472,667
Mfg-Outdoor Products	3949	33992	0.70	1.11	0.30	2,746,000
Mfg-Paint Products	2851	32551	0.66	1.44	0.00	336,333
Mfg-Paper Products	2671	322221	0.49	0.73	0.26	1,833,667
Mfg-Paper Products	2621	322121	0.52	1.11	0.00	2,815,000
Mfg-Pet Bedding	2299	31321	0.65	0.65	0.65	1,735,000
Mfg-Picture Frames	3952	337139	0.33	1.00	0.00	1,013,000
Mfg-Plastic Injection	3089	326199	0.58	0.96	0.19	661,000
Mfg-Plastic Products	3079	326121	0.68	1.27	0.08	2,154,350
Mfg-Popcorn Products	2096	311919	0.87	0.89	0.85	255,500
Mfg-Power Cylinders	3593	33271	0.44	0.44	0.44	9,423,000
Mfg-Power Plant Products	3699	335313	0.66	1.36	0.00	3,472,800
Mfg-Pumps	3561	333912	0.39	0.39	0.39	1,162,000
Mfg-Refrigeration Equipment	3585	333415	0.63	1.43	0.00	2,335,875
Mfg-Roll Shutters	2899	321999	0.46	0.81	0.10	671,500
Mfg-Rubber Aprons	2384	315211	0.30	0.30	0.30	125,000
Mfg-Rubber Pct Products	3069	326299	0.27	0.27	0.27	220,000
Mfg-Screw Machining	3451	332721	0.88	1.60	0.15	1,791,000

Business Description	SIC	NAICS	Average Multiple	Hi	Low	Average Sales
Mfg-Security Systems	3671	334411	0.73	0.73	0.73	1,500,000
Mfg-Sheet metal	3443	332322	0.32	0.56	0.09	1,915,667
Mfg-Signal Processing Equip	3679	334419	0.43	0.43	0.43	2,600,000
Mfg-Snack Foods	2068	311911	0.24	0.24	0.24	750,000
Mfg-Software	7371	541511	0.62	1.28	0.00	1,026,929
Mfg-Solar/Security Film	3081	326113	0.51	0.51	0.51	24,000,000
Mfg-Spa Covers	2394	314912	0.54	1.17	0.00	523,118
Mfg-Specialty Food	2047	311111	0.59	1.50	0.00	493,667
Mfg-Specialty Product	3499	332999	0.59	1.16	0.02	868,824
Mfg-Stereo Speakers	3651	33431	0.54	0.54	0.54	158,000
Mfg-Store Fixtures	2541	337131	0.16	0.26	0.06	2,977,000
Mfg-Styrofoam Products	3086	32615	0.52	0.87	0.17	1,734,286
Mfg-Terrariums	3962	339999	0.37	0.37	0.37	190,000
Mfg-Textile Equipment	3552	33319	0.25	0.25	0.25	4,000,000
MfgTextilePrinting Eq.	3559	333319	0.50	0.61	0.39	4,912,500
Mfg-Tool & Die	3544	333514	0.71	1.17	0.25	2,668,231
Mfg-Tool & Die	3541	333514	0.36	0.57	0.15	641,750
Mfg-Trailers	3721	336212	0.39	0.58	0.19	7,100,000
Mfg-Trophy Awards	5999	453999	0.43	0.87	0.00	512,317
Mfg-Truck Products	3465	33637	0.36	0.36	0.36	610,000
Mfg-Trusses	2439	321214	0.42	0.67	0.17	1,249,333
Mfg-Turquoise Refining	3915	339913	0.33	0.33	0.33	339,000
Mfg-Vibrating Screens	3569	333999	0.87	0.87	0.87	2,900,000
Mfg-Vinyl Notebooks	2678	322233	0.85	0.85	0.85	355,000
Mfg-Weight Loss Suppl	2833	325411	0.43	0.43	0.43	1,410,000
Mfg-Wheel Chairs	3842	339113	1.18	2.21	0.15	504,500
MfgWindMeasur Device	3829	334519	0.86	1.27	0.45	1,937,500
Mfg-Window Coverings	5714	442291	0.41	0.76	0.06	627,667
Mfg-Window Coverings	2591	33792	0.49	0.67	0.31	798,750
Mfg-Windows	2431	321911	0.42	0.93	0.00	1,476,500
Mfg-Windshield Cleaner	2842	325612	0.38	0.74	0.02	949,000
Mfg-Wood Pallets	2448	32192	0.56	1.17	0.00	1,314,000
Mfg-Wood Products	2499	321999	0.46	0.85	0.08	1,599,837
Mfr-Motors/Generators	3621	335312	1.11	1.11	1.11	742,000
Mini-Mart W/Gas/Wash	5541	44711	0.19	0.40	0.00	1,982,132
Mobil Disk Jockey	7929	71119	0.75	0.75	0.75	67,000
Mobile Advertising	7312	54182	0.72	1.33	0.11	401,000
Motorcycle Dealership	5571	441221	0.29	0.64	0.00	3,076,367
Movie Theater-2 Screens	7832	512131	0.36	0.50	0.21	324,667
MRI Examinations	8093	621498	0.49	0.59	0.39	1,046,333
Mud Jacking Service	1389	213113	0.36	0.36	0.36	239,000
Office Equipment Repair	7378	811212	0.43	0.55	0.31	100,500
One Hour Photo	7384	812922	0.59	1.02	0.17	523,333
Parking Lot Sweeping	4959	562998	0.56	0.98	0.13	369,273
Parking Services	7521	812930	0.61	0.61	0.61	383,000
Party Photographers	7221	541921	0.54	1.02	0.06	337,667
Pest Control	7342	56171	0.63	1.19	0.06	213,929
Pet Grooming/Boarding	752	81291	0.63	1.26	0.00	194,767
PhotoStudioLittleLeagues	7335	541922	0.45	0.47	0.44	294,500
Plactic Lamination	3083	32613	0.83	0.83	0.83	226,000

Business Description	SIC	NAICS	Average Multiple	Hi	Low	Average Sales
Plant Grower	181	111421	0.27	0.53	0.00	980,333
Pool Cleaning Service	7389	56179	0.55	1.03	0.06	335,793
Pre-Stress Concrete	3272	32739	0.61	1.11	0.11	922,143
PrintGlueFold Cardboard	2675	322298	0.79	1.29	0.29	640,375
Printing - Forms	2761	323116	0.46	0.46	0.46	800,000
Printing Account Forms	2759	323119	0.51	0.83	0.19	132,500
Printing Shop	2752	323114	0.56	0.97	0.15	638,103
Public Scales	4785	448490	1.48	1.48	1.48	54,000
Radiator Repair Shop	7539	811118	0.44	0.87	0.01	415,438
Radio Broadcasting Station	4832	513112	4.37	7.17	1.56	325,500
RE Sales/Property Man.	6531	53121	0.68	1.33	0.03	532,314
Recreational Park	7033	721211	0.84	2.13	0.00	383,000
Recycling-Anti-Freeze	5093	42193	0.62	1.36	0.00	832,529
Redimix U-Haul Concrete	3273	32732	0.64	1.36	0.00	825,750
Refrigeration Repair	7623	811211	0.51	0.53	0.50	406,500
Remfg-Indust Compressors	3563	333912	0.27	0.55	0.00	288,500
Rental-Cellular Phones	4813	51333	0.54	1.01	0.06	1,286,267
Restr W/Cocktails	5812.009766	72211	0.35	0.64	0.05	766,723
Restr-Asian	5812.069824	722211	0.34	0.60	0.08	851,143
Restr-Breakfast/Lunch	5812.040039	722211	0.41	0.70	0.13	252,421
Restr-Coffee Shop	5812.049805	722211	0.37	0.64	0.09	306,000
Restr-Dinnerhouse	5812.02002	72211	0.36	0.69	0.03	590,944
Restr-Family	5812.029785	722211	0.35	0.61	0.08	598,152
Restr-Greek Food	5812.080078	722211	0.48	0.69	0.27	246,500
Restr-Italian	5812.089844	722211	0.32	0.55	0.10	473,202
Restr-Mexican	5812.100098	722211	0.33	0.57	0.09	401,806
Restr-Seafood	5812.060059	722211	0.30	0.48	0.12	1,037,318
Restr-Vegetarian	5812	722211	0.34	0.43	0.25	233,000
Retail Property Lessors	6512	53112	0.37	0.37	0.37	620,000
Retail/Mail Order-CD?s	5735	45122	0.31	0.31	0.31	258,000
Retail-Appliances	5722	44311	0.40	0.71	0.08	516,143
Retail-Arts & crafts	5945	45112	0.31	0.59	0.03	462,742
Retail-Candy & Nuts	5441	445292	0.37	0.59	0.16	219,417
Retail-Cellular Phones	4812	513321	0.50	0.98	0.02	787,971
RetailChildren?s Furn.	5021	44211	0.28	0.37	0.19	652,000
Retail-Clothing	5621	44812	0.30	0.67	0.00	429,347
Retail-Electronics	5731	44312	0.31	0.46	0.17	741,143
Retail-Fabrics	5949	45113	0.37	0.64	0.11	576,500
Retail-Feed Store	5991	44422	0.22	0.42	0.02	1,964,000
Retail-Floor Coverings	5713	44221	0.30	0.56	0.03	1,079,676
Retail-Florist	5992	45311	0.40	0.68	0.11	301,870
Retail-Furniture	5712	337133	0.29	0.52	0.07	1,097,535
Retail-Garden Store	5261	44422	0.28	0.64	0.00	1,340,556
Retail-Gifts	5947	45322	0.37	0.73	0.01	358,464
Retail-Golf Carts	5088	42186	0.31	0.56	0.06	837,846
Retail-Grocery/Deli	5411	44511	0.28	0.57	0.00	749,733
Retail-Health Products	5499	446191	0.57	1.11	0.02	337,476

185

Business Description	SIC	NAICS	Average Multiple	Hi	Low	Average Sales
Retail-Jewelry	5944	44831	0.60	1.08	0.12	367,600
Retail-Kitchenware	5719	442299	0.46	1.03	0.00	777,474
RetailLawn&Garden Eqt	5086	44421	0.09	0.09	0.09	680,000
Retail-Liquor Store	5921	44531	0.32	0.57	0.07	865,786
Retail-Lumber/Hardware	5211	42131	0.33	0.58	0.08	1,968,500
Retail-Men?s Clothes	5611	44811	0.29	0.43	0.15	774,500
Retail-Music Store	5736	45114	0.26	0.39	0.14	346,286
Retail-Newstand	5994	451212	0.35	0.70	0.00	576,500
Retail-Office Supply	5943	45321	0.28	0.47	0.09	614,167
Retail-Optical Store	5995	44613	0.46	0.84	0.07	503,000
RetailOutdoor Eqt.	5941	45111	0.31	0.62	0.01	600,106
Retail-Pharmacy	5912	44611	0.20	0.31	0.08	1,269,333
Retail-Photo & Cameras	5946	44313	0.12	0.17	0.07	591,500
Retail-Shoes	5661	44821	0.24	0.48	0.01	731,222
Retail-Spas/Billiards	5091	42191	0.37	0.67	0.07	2,064,800
Retail-Sports Apparel	5699	44819	0.30	0.55	0.05	468,304
Retail-Tires & Rims	5531	44132	0.33	0.67	0.00	776,606
Retail-Tobacco Shop	5993	453991	0.20	0.38	0.03	740,300
Retail-Used Clothing	5632	44819	0.40	0.67	0.13	221,667
Retail-Used Office Furn	5932	45331	0.27	0.45	0.08	670,000
Retail-Variety Store	5331	45299	0.33	0.69	0.00	1,397,944
Retail-Wedding Clothes	5821	44812	0.27	0.27	0.27	202,000
Ret-Child Clothes(2Loc)	5641	44813	0.21	0.39	0.03	686,143
Reupholstery Shop	7641	81142	0.46	0.84	0.07	468,632
RV Dealership	5561	44121	0.16	0.26	0.05	3,647,889
Sale/Serv-Air Compr	5082	42181	0.39	0.89	0.00	1,513,375
Sales/Serv-Computers	5734	44312	0.29	0.61	0.00	1,486,071
SalesServElectric Motors	4063	44419	0.46	0.46	0.46	755,000
Sales-Agri/Const Trailers	5599	941229	0.18	0.44	0.00	5,143,500
Secretarial Service	7338	561492	0.52	0.93	0.10	297,472
Ship Repair/Dry Dock	3731	336611	1.39	1.39	1.39	4,325,000
Shoe Repair	7251	81143	0.43	1.30	0.00	49,500
Sign Manufacturer	3993	33995	0.56	0.95	0.17	564,000
Sign Rental & Installation	7390	56179	0.97	0.97	0.97	154,000
Silk Screen Printing	2396	323113	0.51	0.88	0.13	515,756
Ski Lodge	7011	721211	0.60	0.60	0.60	240,000
Soil Decontamination	1629	23493	0.33	0.58	0.09	1,026,667
Spec Medical Practice	8011	621111	0.61	1.17	0.04	744,167
Sports Therapy Center	8049	62134	0.64	0.97	0.31	500,667
Steel Erection	1791	23591	0.38	0.82	0.00	1,849,714
Steel Processing	3325	331513	0.70	0.70	0.70	1,826,000
Storage Lockers	4225	53115	0.80	1.87	0.00	280,333
Swim Club W/Lessons	7941	711211	0.54	0.54	0.54	91,000
Tanning Salon	7299	812199	0.63	1.12	0.15	242,045
Tax and Bookkeeping	8921	541219	0.78	1.27	0.29	222,556
Taxi Cab Fleet	4121	48531	0.44	0.94	0.00	672,000
Telecom Cabling	1623	23492	0.77	1.58	0.00	4,635,462
Telephone Repair	7629	811211	0.28	0.48	0.08	530,750
Title Insurance	6361	524127	0.76	1.34	0.18	621,154
Title Insurance	6541	524127	0.65	0.65	0.65	271,000
Tract Home Builder	1531	23321	0.06	0.06	0.06	10,733,000

Business Description	SIC	NAICS	Average Multiple	Hi	Low	Average Sales
Transportation Consultants	4731	541614	0.50	0.50	0.50	200,000
Trash Containers	4953	562219	1.09	1.91	0.27	539,857
Travel Agency	4724	56151	0.12	0.33	0.00	1,432,118
Travel Tour Operator	4725	56152	0.15	0.30	0.00	3,175,750
Trucking Company	4212	484122	0.67	1.15	0.20	991,500
Typesetting Service	2791	323122	0.64	0.64	0.64	192,000
Used Car Dealer	5521	44112	0.28	0.55	0.00	754,800
Used Lab Equipment	5049	446199	0.36	0.36	0.36	1,814,000
Vending Machines	5962	45421	0.82	1.34	0.29	263,545
Vending-Stuffed Animals	7993	71312	0.63	1.35	0.00	402,500
Veterinary Clinic	742	54194	0.62	0.96	0.29	339,167
Video Tape Duplication	7819	51211	0.79	0.79	0.79	307,000
Video Tape Rental	7841	53223	0.47	0.90	0.05	221,377
Vocational Trade School	8249	611519	0.77	1.49	0.04	452,611
Warehouse & Crating	4226	49311	0.58	0.58	0.58	394,000
Warranty Insur Carriers	6399	524128	0.09	0.09	0.09	147,000
Water Purification	2834	325412	1.62	5.02	0.00	1,309,500
Water Treatment	8999	71151	0.60	1.07	0.14	328,500
Welding Repair Business	7699	81131	0.56	1.10	0.02	356,541
Welding-Trailer Hitches	7692	81149	0.28	0.61	0.00	213,000
Whlse-Tropical Fish	5154	42252	0.10	0.10	0.10	275,000
Whsle-Bakery	5481	311811	0.49	0.78	0.20	246,000
Whsle-Blown Glass	3229	327212	0.27	0.27	0.27	360,000
Whsle-Bread Bakery	2051	311812	0.52	0.87	0.17	596,429
Whsle-Durable Goods	5099	42131	0.43	0.69	0.17	1,109,056
Whsle-Eyeglass Frames	5048	421460	0.38	0.38	0.38	234,000
Whsle-Farm Supplies	5191	42291	0.30	0.65	0.00	998,909
Whsle-HVAC Products	5074	42172	0.37	0.66	0.08	2,033,000
Whsle-Ice Cream	5147	42249	0.25	0.49	0.00	686,400
Whsle-Liquor	5182	42281	0.34	0.34	0.34	746,000
Whsle-Nursery	5193	42293	0.36	0.68	0.05	941,083
Whsle-Produce	5148	42248	0.25	0.53	0.00	2,689,750
Whsle-Seafood	5421	45439	0.27	0.45	0.09	1,315,429
Whsle-Truck Parts	5013	44131	0.33	0.64	0.02	1,026,034
Wireless Telcom	4899	513322	0.45	0.71	0.20	508,750

Chapter 52 Size and Type of Business

This table shows the impact of business size for SIC code 5812 classification of Eating Places. This category includes establishments primarily engaged in the retail sale of prepared food and drinks for on premise or immediate consumption. Caterers and industrial food service establishments are also included in this industry.

This data is from two popular valuation data bases from the Institute of Business Appraisal (IBA) and Pratt Stat's. The Pratt data base typically contains more large businesses compared to IBA. EBIT (Earnings before Interest and Taxes) is similar to the Seller's Discretionary Cash Flow except the owner's compensation is not included in the EBIT cash flow. The multiples shown are the average multiples for the SIC code 5812.

IBA Data 5812	50 to 100K	100K to 500K	500K to $1M	$1M to $5M	$5M to $20M
Price /Sales	0.53	0.40	0.36	0.43	0.65
Price /EBIT	2.61	2.13	3.68	3.33	13.85
Pratt 5812					
Price /Sales	0.58	0.42	0.36	0.38	0.65
Price /EBIT	3.52	4.10	5.44	5.17	8.68

As can be seen the multiples, there is a significant change as the business size is increased.

The other general consideration is that the type of business will greatly impact the multiple and resulting valuation. While restaurants may be the most popular business that is bought and sold, businesses that are in distribution, manufacturing and wholesale products and services are most desirable from an investor's point of view and are highly sought after.

Chaper 53 Buyer Purchase Justification Test

This table shows how a buyer can evaluate the investment in terms of his expected return. As shown the buyer purchases the company for $3,590,000 with a 25% down payment and the rest financed over 10 years.

The resulting cash flow for the first two years is shown with expected earnings of $734,538 the first year and $806,271 the second year. As shown the interest payment and taxes are subtracted as well as the principal payment on the loan.

The resulting after tax cash flow shows a 14.7% return the first year and an 18.9% return the second year.

Estimate of Value - Company Only	3,590,000
Cash Down Payment (25%)	897,500
Amount Financed by Seller/Bank (10 Years @ 8%)	2,692,500
First Year of Forecast:	
Adjusted Pretax Net Income	734,538
Less: Interest Payment @ 8%	208,778
Taxable Income	525,759
Less: 40% Tax Rate	210,304
Subtotal	315,456
Less: Principal Payment	183,231
Cash Flow	132,224
Note: Cash on Cash Return (On Down Payment)	14.7%
Second Year of Forecast:	
Adjusted Pretax Net Income	806,271
Less: Interest Payment @ 8%	193,570
Taxable Income	612,701
Less: 40% Tax Rate	245,080
Subtotal	367,620
Less: Principal Payment	198,439
Cash Flow	169,181
Note: Cash on Cash Return (On Down Payment)	18.9%

If you are a buyer it is important that you forecast your expected cash flow and target return you want to achieve for the investment.

Chapter 54 Business App Software

There are software apps that can help you selling or buying a business. They are extremely useful and worth the time and expense of using them in your acquisition process. These apps are available on Windows, iPhone and iPad as designated below. They have been developed by Openview Publishing and have been distributed for the last four years to thousands of users. You can download them from the Windows Store or the Apple App Store. Just search for the app name in the store.

As designated below there are apps that are available in the Apple App Store. In the Apple App Store you can search for the name Openview Publishing to see all apps and select from that list or you can enter the name of the app and search for it. The apps that are designed SP are specially designed for the iPad.

Business Buy Sell (Windows Store – desktop)

The app estimates the fair market value of your company. It is based on the Market Approach to business valuation which is the most widely used and accurate method to value a business. The program also contains the Factor Method used by many Business Brokers. This Market Approach uses actual market transactions as a basis for comparison. It is the most fundamental approach in a fair market value appraisal and it is said by many that this is the only practical approach to Business Valuation. There are those who propose to use Rules of Thumb, however it is generally accepted among appraisers that these comparisons are static and do not reflect the market conditions. It also contains an extensive tutorial on buying and selling a business.

- Tutorial and Reference Guide on buying and selling a business
- Business Value by Market Approach
- Data base of Market Multiples
- Business Value by Factor Method
- You can study up to 200 different businesses
- Maintains a data base of SIC code descriptions and codes
- Full Reporting of results
- Selling your Business Functions
- Buying a Business Cash Flow Analysis
- Buying a Business Negotiator

My Capital Gain (iPhone and iPad)

You own a house, maybe you own a business or commercial property. You may be wondering, if I sell how much will I get? How much goes to Uncle Sam? How can I be sure? This App shows you the money! With a few inputs it cranks through the calculation and give you the answer in black and white.

Business Buy Sell (iPhone) and Business Buy Sell SP (iPad)

If you are a business owner, someone who wants to buy a business or someone who wants to sell a business you need to buy this app. It contains functions that will allow you to determine the value of a business – the starting place for buying or selling a business. It is comprehensive, it was designed and written by Certified Business Brokers and Appraisers. It will save you thousands, maybe even millions of dollars.

If you are a seller, it answers the age old question – how much am I going to get after I sell my company? It calculates your gain, your taxes and your proceeds.

If you are a Buyer, it will calculate your cash flows after debt service and contains your own personal negotiator function to allow you to quickly study numerous purchasing alternatives.

It contains three unique features; a report generator and email capability for emailing reports and it includes the ability to study 30 individual businesses.

Biz Value (iPhone) and Biz Value SP (iPad)

This is the perfect app for business owners and business brokers. It contains two unique features; a report generator and email capability for emailing reports.

BizValue estimates the fair market value of your company. It is based on the Market Approach to business valuation which is the most widely used and accurate method to value a business. The program also contains the

Factor Method used by many Business Brokers. This Market Approach uses actual market transactions as a basis for comparison. It is the most fundamental approach in a fair market value appraisal and it is said by many that this is the only practical approach to Business Valuation. There are those who propose to use Rules of Thumb, however it is generally accepted among appraisers that these comparisons are static and do not reflect the market conditions. It is easy to use and thorough. It has been developed by Certified Business Appraisers.

Services Provided by Author

As part of Horton Business Group the author provides services throughout the United States. These services include:

- Business Valuation for the seller or buyer
- Finder's Service – marketing your company for sale, finding a buyer and negotiations of a deal
- Due Diligence Services – consulting support to the buyer during due diligence

In Florida the Horton Business group will find a buyer for both your business and property associated with it. See our website www.hortonbrokers.com

Contact us at email hortonbrokers@aol.com

We provide services to realtors, sellers and buyers.

If are a realtor and have a business you want to sell you can refer it to us or we can work with you directly to get the business valued, marketed and sold.

If you are a seller we will value your business, find buyers, prequalify them and help you negotiate a deal and if you are a buyer we can help you find the right business and help you negotiate the right deal.

Please contact us we can send a proposal for services right away.

About the Author

BS Louisiana State University
MS and MBA University of Tennessee
Ph.D. Virginia Tech
Licensed Broker by the Florida Real Estate Commission
Certified Business Intermediary
Certified Business Appraiser

He was the owner and founder of consulting firm providing project management and financial assistance to clients throughout the world owned and operated two multimillion dollar software companies. He was the Manager and Director of international consulting firm. Dr. Horton has owned, operated and started several high tech businesses in the past twenty-five years. During this time his experiences encompassed all phases of business operation including production, legal, taxes, marketing and development. Dr. Horton negotiated the sale of his largest company to a publicly traded billion dollar corporation and has provided consultation to other business owners on the sale of their companies for the last thirteen years. Dr. Horton has many years of experience performing forensic accounting on seller's financials, analysis of financials during due diligence phase of acquisition and business valuation.

Dr. Horton is also a highly decorated veteran having served as an infantry sergeant in Vietnam.